PREACHING AT THE PARISH COMMUNION
ASB GOSPELS—SUNDAYS; YEAR TWO

Also by CANON RAYMOND WILKINSON:
My Confirmation Search-Book
An Adult Confirmation Candidate's Handbook

PREACHING
AT THE PARISH
COMMUNION

ASB Gospels—Sundays: Year Two

CANON RAYMOND WILKINSON
Rector of Solihull
Chaplain to H.M. The Queen

MOWBRAY
LONDON & OXFORD

First published 1983
by A. R. Mowbray & Co. Ltd
Saint Thomas House, Becket Street,
Oxford, OX1 1SJ

Typeset by Preface Ltd, Salisbury, Wilts.
Printed in Great Britain by R. J. Acford Ltd., Chichester

TO DOROTHY, my wife;
and FRANCIS, ANDREW, MARK and PAUL, our sons;
against which supportive family background
these thoughts have matured through
the years.

ACKNOWLEDGEMENTS

I am deeply indebted to many retreat conductors, preachers and writers who have inspired me over the years. My rough notebooks only occasionally give the source of words which have helped me and which have become part of me. Where possible, these sources are acknowledged.

I owe more than I can ever say to those who have listened to me over the years and have encouraged me to fresh efforts in ministry, especially in preaching.

Finally I record my grateful thanks to Kitty Freck, who patiently took my dictation at all sorts of odd times.

R.S.W.

Most biblical passages are from the New English Bible, unless otherwise stated.

FOREWORD

This book of sermon outlines is the work of a parish priest through and through. It is the product of years and years of caring for people as a father-in-God; and not only caring for them, but understanding them. It comes out of an exceptionally busy life. Does he not tell us in one sermon that he has prepared one thousand candidates for confirmation in ten years? What must be the other demands made upon a pastor with responsibilities of this dimension!

That these sermons do derive from such a *Sitz im Leben* (life situation) will be evident to all who read them, and the work I have had to do on them as Series Editor has not blurred this important fact. Because it is important. These books are designed to assist priests and pastors with their preaching ministries. Preaching properly understood is part of the pastoral office. How fitting then that one book in this series—and not the only one—should arise hot from a pastoral situation. And how right that this one should come from the Catholic wing of the Church, and reflect it unashamedly.

D. W. CLEVERLEY FORD

CONTENTS

PREFACE

In each of the varied parishes where I have served and which have meant so much to my family and me, I have tried to hold in balance the Word and the Sacraments, as befits a priest of the Church of England.

The importance of preaching cannot be overstressed; though, patently, you cannot preach unless you have a message, and also a real desire to communicate it. Over and over again it needs to be stressed that there is much need for simple words to be the vehicle of God's truth. The sermon forms a substantial part of the image of the clergyman; the stage parson will almost certainly include a demonstration of preaching. Our faithful laity may express the hope that the sermon will not be too long and make untoward remarks about its contents. Yet still lives can be changed by preaching, even though the preacher concerned may never know the result of his words.

When the preacher ascends the pulpit, he is in a sense exhibiting the Crucified. He stands helpless before the crowd; his inadequate words often fall on deaf ears. In the congregation there will be those who, like the Jews, seek a sign; those who, like the Greeks, are looking for wisdom; but we preach Christ crucified.

We have been given that commission by God himself; and as our message is the Word of God and not the opinions of men, no apology is called for from those who prepare themselves properly for this great part of our ministry.

Solihull Rectory,   RAYMOND WILKINSON
West Midlands.

NINTH SUNDAY BEFORE CHRISTMAS

God's Healing Work

> John 3.5 *'No one can enter the Kingdom of God without being born from water and spirit.'*

Today the theme for our readings is the creation. So we begin with the nature of God himself, because it all begins with God. I wish we *could* all believe that everything begins with God. If only we could get back to God at the beginning of the day; get back to God at the beginning of any enterprise; to let it, that is to say, all begin with God—in all our thinking and in all our planning and in all our attempts to probe and understand the mysteries of the universe and the meaning of life—to begin, not with ourselves, but with God, as the Bible does. The very first words in the Bible are, 'In the beginning God . . .' That is the place to start.

1 *God at work*

All the truth that surrounds and supports the Church's claim to the commission, which we believe Jesus Christ gave to us—it all begins with God, with his nature and with his character. What do we know about him? First, that the Bible reveals God as being active always in three ways; God is creating and redeeming and sanctifying. Wherever we see God at work we see him making something or re-making something so that it may be perfect. Consequently, we think of him as creator, father, redeemer, sanctifier; and when St John talks about God in his epistles he brings to us the essential thought of God, that *God is love*. Now love is not just a sentimental idea; it is an active thing. Love is always at work. We know this from our experience of love in a close family. It is always at work, doing that which is good for somebody else.

Bishop Westcott of Durham said, 'Love is the spontaneous planning for someone else's good.' So whenever you are at work for somebody else, whenever your prayers are concerned with the restoration of someone else's life or personality or health of body or mind, then there is God.

2 God at work everywhere

And now something else about God. God is everywhere. We do not have to make a journey to any particular place to be in touch with God. We do not necessarily have to come to church because we believe that God is here. Of course God is here, and I have no doubt that God is particularly here; but God is always about us. We can always be in touch with him—on the way to work in the morning, in the train, in the office, in the home, everywhere. God is spirit and, therefore, God is immediately and everywhere available. So this power, this love, this redemption, which is God, is always here. To use an example from the body, if you cut your finger and it becomes infected, then the whole body organizes itself to bring to bear upon the wound all the energy available in the body to heal it. The whole body co-operates to heal. In the same way God is always about us; available, redeeming, cleansing, forgiving and loving. He is there to meet our need and to restore our personality to wholeness and soundness and goodness.

3 Our needs for which God works

(a) Healing

When Jesus came to earth, a very large part of his work was concerned with healing the minds and bodies of men. This is behind his conversation with Nicodemus in today's Gospel, when he says, 'No one can enter the kingdom of God without being reborn.' 'It is spirit,' he says, 'that gives birth to spirit.' We see Jesus at work giving men back what they have lost—to the blind their sight, to the deaf their hearing, to the leper a clean body, to the dead life, to the diseased in mind the freedom from the power of evil.

2

Wherever he was, he re-created human life. You remember the threefold commission, 'Go and preach the Gospel; cast out evil spirits; lay hands on the sick and they shall recover.' Wherever there is a church today those three activities ought to be going on.

(b) Forgiveness
Jesus made possible the joy of forgiveness. When someone is beaten down with despondency, failure and brokenness, what can be offered in such an hour of awareness of need except that God has made it possible for forgiveness to be granted? No person is really changed until there is knowledge of forgiveness, because only then can he be restored.

(c) Disobedience
Perhaps the greatest need of all as we consider the revival of the healing ministry in the life of the Church is to ask ourselves, 'Why have I this disease? Why am I asthmatic? Why have I this ulcer?' It is certainly true that many will find that the reason is not medical, not physical, but moral, rooted in some disobedience, found in some sin which we have refused to allow God to deal with. So when Jesus healed those who came to him he said, 'Go and sin no more, lest a worse thing come to you.' 'I say to you your sins are forgiven.' So in St James: 'Confess your faults that you may be healed.' The psychosomatic results are incalculable. Laying hands upon the sick ought to be a normal practice in every parish church, for the sick to come in and receive the healing touch of the hand of Christ.

Application

So we today think of the world in all its need. Its need of healing on the international level; its need of healing industrially; of all the broken homes needing healing; of all the broken hearts that need binding up; of the sick bodies that need the healing touch of Christ. And we think of God, who when he creates something always makes it 'good', and when it goes wrong redeems it, and the Church as his

3

healing agency. Finally, and perhaps above all in these days, we think of man in his disobedience, of man and his need, of man and his sin, and, if you bring these together, recall some words from the fifteenth chapter of Exodus, 'for I the Lord am your healer.'

EIGHTH SUNDAY BEFORE CHRISTMAS

The Sin of Unfaithfulness

> John 3.17 '*It was not to judge the world that God sent his Son into the world, but that through him the world might be saved.*'

We should think of suffering, not as something sent to us, but as an experience belonging to our human nature. So suffering is an experience in which we all share, directly or indirectly. Many who face troubles are worried, not because they are having to suffer, but because they cannot say why.

1 *The suffering unfaithfulness produces*

We know that physical pain is only one form of suffering. We have a mind and a spirit, too, and so we need not be surprised that those parts of us can suffer even more than our bodies. I once heard a friend of mine say that he didn't think bodily pain was a serious problem at all. As he was a Christian doctor, I paid attention to what he said, and he backed up his statement by saying that there is a limit to the amount of pain that our nerves can feel. Of course, pain can be frightening, and many do wonder just how much more they can bear. But physical pain has a physical cause; and, once we know what it is, then the pain loses its worst terror. We can even look at it with a kind of detachment and hold on until relief comes. The worst part, and what can be so terrifying, is the fear of the unknown and the unexplained; this is especially so in cases of mental distress or anxiety. The circumstances may differ, of course, but I have found myself faced over and over again in my ministry with the problem of unfaithfulness of husband and wife—the problem of the broken marriage, the broken home and, what the Bible calls quite bluntly, adultery.

This sort of suffering is due far more to our sins against one another than to anything else. Often, when faced with suffering which has been caused directly by one person sinning against another and the injured person says, 'Why does God allow this?', then I am sure we have got to accept two simple facts. One is that God does not want this sort of thing to happen, and the other that it does happen because one person has sinned against another. I still believe that God can use suffering for a great and wonderful purpose. The kind of suffering caused by unfaithfulness makes it appear that a whole lifetime of care and thought and love has been trampled on, and that we face a quite hopeless situation. Of course, it is difficult to face such facts, and any sweeping statements are bound to be insufficient, but there are certain things to keep in mind—things which, if we hold on to them, will stand good always. We have to remember that against the modern background, which has seen such an increase in broken marriages, nevertheless, for every instance of people being unfaithful and causing unhappiness to others, there are thousands the other way, who are faithful and with happiness holding firm.

2 *The happiness faithfulness produces*

Preparing young people for their marriages is one of the most wonderful things that any parish priest is called upon to do; and it is a great privilege to witness the high hopes with which they enter into the married state, and the lovely homes that so many of them set up. We hear much of the marriages that are wrecked. We must never forget the great majority of solid marriages that we don't hear much about. We hear of sordid passions of adultery and misery; we mustn't forget the sweetness and happiness of a love that grows stronger and purer as life goes on. In other words, if it has happened to us, this great sorrow of heart, we really must try very hard to keep things in their right perspective. It may sound almost silly at first, if you are unhappy, for it to be suggested that you can try and think of the many others who are happy. In a way, of course, it makes it even harder to bear our own loss, when we think of the happiness that could and should have been ours too; but although it is one of the hardest things to bear, we can learn to rejoice over goodness, truth and beauty, wherever they are to be found, just because they are good things, and we are glad to know that they are there.

In fact, we get very near to the spirit of Christ himself when we can actually thank God, not because *we* are happy, but because there is no much happiness and good-ness still in this world. When we do this, we begin to share that happiness, because it comes to us as well. It is, perhaps, the purest form of joy that there is, to be able to rejoice over the happiness that others have even when we haven't it ourselves. The finest kind of joy is free from all selfishness.

3 *The need to avoid bitterness*

The sorrow that is inflicted on the heart of another by unfaithfulness is one of the most humiliating of all sor-rows, because we have loved and trusted another person, and now we feel that that love and trust have been be-trayed and that in some way we are a failure. We cannot possibly believe that this was what God intended. It cannot be God's will that anyone should so behave towards another person. What is the will of God now? The thing has happened, so the question is, 'What does God want me to do about it; and can any good possibly come out of it?' There is one thing we certainly can do. We can refuse to let ourselves be embittered by this experience. If this is the case, one of the finest things that can come out of it is a great sympathy for other people who have suffered in the same way. I am quite sure that the people who have done most to fight against the evils that cause suffering, have been the people who have been through it themselves.

One of the finest priests that I know came from a very bad home indeed, and he had the grace to learn many lessons from the experience and to apply great quantities of healing balm in other such families. I think of the great Japanese social reformer, Kagawa; his home life was terribly unhappy and his early days broken by suffering and shame. Instead of becoming embittered and resentful, he dedicated his life to fighting those very evils that brought such suffering to him. Millions of Japanese people, directly or indirectly, owe their happiness to him. He was just following the example of Christ in all that he did. So there is a very definite way in which we can turn personal suffering and unhappiness to good account. Simply by refusing to be embittered by it we are actually helping other people. If they know what has happened and still find us charitable and generous in our judgement, they will be encouraged to believe in what is good and true and lovely in life.

Conclusion

Unfaithfulness is a sin and it brings in its wake many sorrows, as so many know only too well. Our Gospel, however, tells of forgiveness. Judgment is never the final word. Listen to the text again with which I began. 'It was not to judge the world that God sent his Son into the world, but that through him the world might be saved.'

SEVENTH SUNDAY BEFORE CHRISTMAS

The way back to God

Luke 20.14 *'This is the heir,' they said; 'let us kill him so that the property may come to us.'*

1 *The Problem*

Many people look upon the amazing wonder of the world and find it hard to understand that there are those who cannot see God behind it all; but besides the wonder there is also the perplexity—the painful perplexity—because there is so much evil present in God's good world. Sickness and suffering, sorrow and selfishness, lust and greed, cruelty and every kind of crime, spoil the good. Evil badly tarnishes the wonder; and whilst undoubtedly it has its effect in nature, the sad fact is that the moral quality of evil appears to stem from man and the wrong choices that he makes. Oddly enough, man, the crown of creation, brings down everything with him in his fall.

People scorn religion. They think they know it all, and they scoff at the garden of Eden parable in the Book of Genesis. They would further scoff at the parable, which stems from it and which is our Gospel for today. This scorn however changes when men and women find God. Then they realize that the 'old serpent, the devil,' enters the garden of their own souls. Hell is the realization of how much we want God and yet are cut off from him.

2 *The Remedy*

If that is the problem, then the remedy is clearly shown for the Christian. Instead of wiping out the human race, God promised it a saviour, who would come and redeem it from the power of sin and help it back to God. Today's parable summarizes what happened. From the moment man first sinned God began preparing the way back. It was bound to take a long time, involving love and patience.

8

Man must first want to be forgiven; and that depends upon his coming to need God and so learning to love God. The Old Testament tells the story of the final and principal stages of this preparation. It may have been 'odd of God to choose the Jews' to be the first members of his teacher training college; but did he not know best? When God considered that man ought to have been ready for the final lesson about himself, he came to earth and was born as the child of a virgin Jewess, named Mary. In this human way God tried to teach man more about himself; in particular, that God is love and longs for man's love. But the lesson was almost too simple. Man cannot grasp humility like this.

So God played his ace. He allowed man to crucify him, with no reproach but rather a prayer of loving forgiveness. Christ died on the cross so that man might learn in this final effort the awfulness of sin (which could even stoop to murder him); and the unquenchable love God had for man, even when a sinner.

3 The necessary response

So Christ's death made it possible for us to be reunited with God, but not automatically. It can only be given if and when it is wanted. To receive the benefits of Christ's redemption, we must go to the foot of the cross and frankly tell him how sorry we are for the things that we have done wrong. Our repentance must be inspired by love of God and not fear. It must also intend amendment of life and the attempt to avoid further sin.

If our repentance is made within the sacramental framework God has provided in his Church, we shall hear his absolving words, giving us the full and complete assurance of forgiveness as well as grace to amend. Then we may go on our way rejoicing.

SIXTH SUNDAY BEFORE CHRISTMAS

The Church of England at risk

> Mark 13.13 *'All will hate you for your allegiance to me; but the man who holds out to the end will be saved.'*

1 *The Church of England*

We may look at this stark warning within the context of the whole Catholic Church. Today also we look at it in the context of the Church of England. We think of those who love it, those who tolerate it, those who wish it were not there. One of the most important things about the Church of England is that you can't join it. We often hear reference to 'members of the Church of England', but there is no such person as a member of the Church of England, for the Church of England is not based on membership. The reason for this is that the Church of England is not a sect or a religious club, but simply and solely the Church as it has arrived in this country and taken root here. The Church of England did not begin to exist at the Reformation or when St Augustine of Canterbury came here in 597. It began to come into existence when Jesus called his first disciples, and it reached its fulfilment on that day of Pentecost, when the Holy Spirit was given to the followers of Jesus and they ceased to be a society of friends and became the Church—the greatest and most significant society that the world has ever seen.

In course of time and in the providence of God the Church came to our country and has remained here for many centuries. We pray that its work and witness will continue until the return of our Lord Jesus Christ in glory. The Church in its entirety, the Body of Christ, the temple of the Holy Spirit, will most certainly last until the day of final victory, because our Lord Jesus has promised that the gates of Hades shall not prevail against it. It is, however, by no means certain that each and every part of the Church will survive.

The Church of North Africa of the early centuries, that great Church of Tertullian, Cyprian and Augustine, perished utterly. The same thing could happen to the Church of England, not through Moslem invasion but through secularist absorption; not through a Donatist schism but through its opposite, a so-called scheme of union, so comprehensive that the Church of England would no longer be recognizable as the Church which St Athanasius and St Augustine and the apostles knew. In such a case it might survive as a philanthropic institution, mainly concerned with raising money for the third world, or a pleasant setting for choruses. But it would no longer be the Church, and we would have to find another name for it.

2 *Two mortal dangers*

(a) Doctrinal

It seems clear that the Church of England is exposed today to two mortal dangers, which may be described in broad terms as doctrinal and institutional. There is a tendency to deny, to abandon or to explain away the fundamental doctrines of our faith. The most important of all Christian doctrines is that of the incarnation, God becoming flesh in the person of Jesus Christ. It is the most important doctrine, because every other doctrine is related to it. Without it, Christianity soon degenerates into a vague and sentimental theism. It is important to notice that the incarnation is rejected by Judaism, Islam, Hinduism and Buddhism and also is wholly unacceptable to the outlook of the modern world.

The incarnation means that God has spoken fully, finally and completely in Jesus Christ. It means that the Word, which God spoke in creation and revelation, was made flesh in Jesus Christ. The classic expression of this doctrine is found in the formulae of Nicaea and Chalcedon, but these only make explicit what is already implicit in the

New Testament statements regarding Jesus Christ. Sit down with your Bible and make a list of all the names and titles applied to Jesus Christ, and then extend your list to include all the terms by which it is anticipated in the Old Testament. You will soon perceive that, as that great scholar Bishop Westcott said, it is the same God who is the author of both revelations, and that a straight line leads from the Bible to Chalcedon. You can also prolong the exercise by working out how the incarnation is related to the doctrine of God on the one hand and to those of the Church and the sacraments on the other hand. You will then be in a position to appreciate how an attack on the doctrine of the incarnation is an attack on Christianity itself. Those who reject the incarnation will not scruple to reject the doctrine of the atonement and the resurrection. Such rejecters will have nothing left to preach except some kind of trendy Marxism, which certainly will have nothing to do with the true theology of the Church of God.

(b) Institutional

The institutional danger arises from a panic cry for reunion at all costs. Reunion is a great and high ideal, for which we must all continue to pray and work, but there is growing a desire for amalgamation for amalgamation's sake, in an attempt to impress the world. It is probable that the world would be as greatly interested in a union between two Christian bodies as it would be in a merger between Marks & Spencer's and Woolworth's. What we have to ask ourselves is what kind of effect institutional or organizational uniting would have upon the Church of England. Would it still be the Church, or would it become something new?

3 *A Church worth preserving*

To say this is in no way to pass judgement upon any other Church. They have their own ways of claiming doctrinal and historic continuity. What is simply being said is that the Church of England is different, distinctive and in some ways unique; Anglicanism with its particular form of faith and order, which the Church of England has given to the world, is most certainly worth preserving. Let us recognize also that, as we pray and work for unity, we must be prepared to be led by the Holy Spirit, to whom we pray. There is a great tendency today that, having prayed to the Holy Spirit for guidance, we then reject his counsel if it happens not to appeal to the decisions which the world is very keen on being arrived at because of expediency.

FIFTH SUNDAY BEFORE CHRISTMAS

Doctrine first

> Mark 13.22 *'Imposters will come claiming to be messiahs or prophets . . . But you be on your guard.'*

1 *Ethics versus Doctrine*

There is apparent today a widespread aversion to doctrinal preaching and teaching, especially against teaching which might lead to commitment to the person of Christ. This aversion is to be found even amongst churchgoers. Questions relating to Christian doctrine are usually regarded as being of little use. The purpose of religion is assumed to be to present to us an ideal of human conduct and continually to exhort us to strive after that ideal. A good Christian is held to be one who does the right kind of things. It is often alleged, 'It doesn't matter what a man believes so long as he lives the right kind of life'; in other words it is claimed that what really matters for religion is that man's outward acts shall be such as to win approval from his fellows.

2 *The collapse of moral standards*

Now, even if Christianity were no more than a scheme for right living, it would still be of inestimable value for the world. Man seems to have a fatal facility for continuously lowering his moral standards; and conduct, which one generation firmly condemns, often tends to become first tolerated and then accepted by the next generation.

At the beginning of this century it was widely held that man, left to himself, must inevitably progress to the attainment of a higher and nobler mode of living. For such writers as H. G. Wells it was the new light round the corner; and man, splendid fellow, was safely on the road to inevitable progress. We see today how that confident prediction has been totally falsified in the most startling manner by the march of history. Civilisation has not advanced; it has collapsed in the most catastrophic manner. It may well sometimes seem that the new Jerusalem of man's creating will be even more tragic than the old Jerusalem has become.

The bitter fact, which we ought to have learned by now, is that man simply cannot work out his own salvation. The possession of a university degree certainly does not make a man one whit less selfish; man does not make inevitable progress towards higher and better things. On the contrary, all experience teaches us that man invariably tends to debase life's experiences. In a world where moral standards are crashing to the ground, it is surely of first importance that religion, even viewed solely as a moral signpost, shall present to man an inflexible standard of moral value; and the constant witness of Christianity to worthy standards of human conduct is of no small value to a world, which is rapidly rejecting all moral standards whatsoever.

3 *The authority of moral law*

Yet, the awkward question arises as to why we should acknowledge as binding any standards at all? Is the moral law, as some now contend, merely the judgement of the community as to what conduct is expedient or otherwise? Because, if this is so, then the moral law can have no final authority, because public opinion changes.

But, if the authority behind the moral law is not the

judgement of the community, what else can it be? Why, in other words, should I feel an obligation to do some things because they are 'right', and to avoid some things because they are 'wrong'? The answer of Christianity to this question is very clear and definite. It is that the basis of the moral law is not the judgement of the community but the will of God. The moral law, like the mass of physical laws which hedge in our earthly lot, is imposed upon us from without, not created by our own corporate judgement. We have no more authority over the moral law than we have over the law of gravity, because both alike are ordained by God.

If that is so, then we are concerned no longer with a code, but with a person, and it is of the utmost importance that we should know as much as possible about that person, whose will impinges on our lives with such force and such frequency. The whole structure of right and wrong hinges upon him. We need, therefore, to know who or what he is—in what ways we can enter into a right relationship with him; and at once we are caught up in a faith, not just a set of rules: a faith in a person. It is this body of truths about God—his nature, his characteristics, his will for and his dealings with man—which goes by the name of Christian doctrine. This is not, as is so often supposed, an unnecessary and rather mysterious department of a religion whose sole legitimate concern is conduct. On the contrary, it is the very ground and foundation of that religion, and the source from which Christian morality itself derives its validity.

Conclusion

The Christian moral law does not and cannot exist by itself, but it is essentially loving obedience to a person, whose nature and being it is the purpose of Christian doctrine to reveal.

15

ADVENT SUNDAY

The Second Coming

> Matthew 25.31 *'When the Son of Man comes in his glory and all the angels with him, he will sit in state on his throne, with all the nations gathered before him.'*

1 *A New Testament expectation*

All through the New Testament there sounds deeply and solemnly the note of expectation. Christian men were looking forward to the second coming of Christ, and we see at once a marked difference between the Christianity of those days and that of our own day, in which this note is rarely heard. In the New Testament we hear it everywhere. In the First Letter to the Corinthians St Paul told the story of the institution of the Eucharist the night before Jesus died in these words, 'For every time you eat this bread and drink the cup, you proclaim the death of the Lord, until he comes' (1 Corinthians 11.26). Every celebration of the Eucharist looks forward to the coming of Christ.

After St John's Gospel was finished another chapter was added, the twenty first, one purpose of which was to explain what exactly Jesus had said to St Peter about St John, 'If it should be my will that he wait until I come, what is it to you?' (John 21.22). The writer points out that this does not necessarily mean that St John would live until our Lord's return—'only if it is my wish'—but we can see how full the minds of those early Christians were of the thought of Jesus coming again. Once more, at the very end of the last book of the Bible, we have the ascended Christ speaking to John in a vision and giving his message to the Church (Revelation 22.20), 'He who gives this testimony speaks: "Yes, I am coming soon!"'; and the seer, speaking for the persecuted Church, replies, 'Amen. Come, Lord Jesus!' So the last words of the New Testament are a prayer for the speedy coming of Christ.

(a) To be realized forthwith
It is quite certain that the first disciplines expected that Christ would come again during their own lifetime. They thought that he would appear almost immediately. St Paul in the earliest piece of writing in the New Testament, his Letter to the Thessalonians, seems to think this. The main subject of that epistle is the second advent and how to behave in preparation for it. Later on, as the years went by and Christ did not come, his mind changed on the subject. Probably the early disciples would have acknowledged that our Lord did not actually tell them that he would come again so soon. They might remember also those striking words of his (Mark 13.32), 'But about that day or that hour no one knows, not even the angels in heaven, not even the Son; only the Father.' So no one, not even Jesus, knew when the return would be; but still the early Christians, with childlike simplicity, thought he said he would come again soon. What people desire very much they like to think will soon be theirs.

(b) To be realized in due time
The years passed and Christ did not come. Some began to question and to murmur. So, in 2 Peter 3.4, we read of some who are asking scornfully, 'Where now is the promise of his coming?', and the writer tries to satisfy the doubter (2 Peter 3.8), 'With the Lord one day is like a thousand years and a thousand years like one day.' In other words, what seems a long time to us is not a long time to God. Still the years went on and lengthened into centuries, and the Lord did not come. The Church found that she must learn to wait, to watch, to work and to pray; that she must strive to bring Christ's kingdom upon earth, whilst always holding the promise of her Lord's return. She has done this and has devoted one season of her year to the consideration of this his hope. In this season of Advent, as we prepare to celebrate the Saviour's first coming at Christmastide, we are called to think also of his second coming at the great day.

2 *A temptation to be resisted*

There is always a temptation, when people have an active belief in the second advent, to make theories as to when it will happen. This is very unwise, and none of these theories can possibly be right. We know they cannot be right because we are told quite definitely that no one knows when the great day will be. Christ said even the angels did not know, any more than the Son himself; and that should be enough for us. Yet men are always constructing their theories as to the day and the hour, and time always proves those theories wrong. Nine centuries after the early Christians had thought Christ was returning, there was a revival of the belief that his arrival was imminent; but he did not come.

In modern times there are people who tell us they have deduced from the Bible the exact year of Christ's coming. Many of the dates indicated by these theories are already past, for various years throughout the nineteenth century were so designated. Still there are prophets who assure us when our Lord will come again. They have worked it out from the Bible itself. They have calculated it from certain mysterious numbers in the Book of Daniel or they have reached their results by elaborate mathematical operations based upon certain measurements of the great pyramid. No doubt these people are quite sincere in their belief, but we shall do well to give no heed to them. As history has demolished previous theories of this sort, so it will demolish theirs. To use the Bible in this way is to vulgarize it and to turn it into a sort of puzzle book. The Bible was not given for this purpose. It is a preposterous use of the holy scripture, which was given to us to help us grow in faith and love and holiness of life and certainly not to puzzle out beforehand what God has kept hidden from us.

But whilst we ought to discourage this kind of improper prediction of the date of Christ's return, nevertheless we should hold our Advent hope firmly and strongly. We *do* believe that Christ will come again in glory to be our judge, even though we have no idea of *when* that time will

18

be, nor *how* he will come. In the New Testament we have vivid pictures of the judge coming on the clouds, surrounded by angelic hosts. These are only pictures, but they set the truth before us in the way in which we can best receive it.

3 *God's advent not man's evolution*

There are two ways in which it is possible for us to think of our Lord's coming. We may call them the way of development and the way of cataclysm. The way of development means the Christian Gospel spreading throughout the world and then, as a last link in the chain of development, Christ manifesting himself in visible presence amongst us. There is a good deal in the Bible to suggest such a beautiful and orderly development, leading up to the reign of God on earth, which the prophets saw in vision.

But then there is the other way of looking at the matter, which seems to be more in accordance with the teaching of Christ himself. It is that the coming of Christ will be a sudden breaking-in upon the world; that the second coming will be a tremendous, overwhelming event, possibly in a world which has become very imperfectly a religious one. It is to be noted that our Lord does not tell us that the whole world will be converted before he comes. He does say that the Gospel will be preached everywhere, but it certainly does not follow that all will accept that Gospel. He will come suddenly, unexpectedly, as a thief in the night, and his advent will be a cataclysm of deliverance to the faithful and the overthrow of the unfaithful. In this connection it is worth remembering that no prophet had ever hinted at the possibility of the Messiah of God coming as a little child born in a stable. We may be sure that that will be equally true of the manner of his second coming.

If we consulted a professor of history, he would probably tell us that the subject of human history is the evolution of mankind. For the Christian, we do not believe that

19

such a statement reveals the real secret of the story of human history. All human history, the Christian believes, is the story of the *coming* into the world, not merely the evolution of man, but the advent of God; *that* is the real and true subject of human history. It is the story of God coming to win his children to himself; coming in prophets and teachers and lawgivers of all races; coming in great happenings of history, the destruction of Jerusalem, the fall of the Roman empire, the shattering of Christendom, of the Reformation, the collapse of nineteenth and twentieth century thinking in the great wars that we have experienced. The story tells also of the coming of God in the incarnation of Jesus Christ and of his coming in the Church, which is the Body of Christ.

4` *The unfinished story*

The story is not yet finished. God has not yet fully come. He has come fully in one sense in that he has given the full and complete revelation of himself in our Lord Jesus Christ, but not yet fully in the sense that there are vast numbers of the human race to whom the Gospel of Christ has not yet been presented. What we have to understand is that all that is happening in the world today is a continuation of what we read in the Bible and in our histories.—Abraham leaving his home at the call of God; Moses giving the people the law of God; Isaiah teaching the men of his day the majesty and holiness of God; our Lord lying as a little child in the manger and as a man dying on the Cross; St Paul preaching the Gospel in Athens or Ephesus; St Augustine bringing that same Gospel to England; missionaries proclaiming that same Gospel in parts of Central Africa and little Indian villages. These are all the same story with the same subject, the advent of God.

The story will be finished one day when Christ comes again, and that will be when all things are ready for him. We may believe that by our loyalty, by our faithful witness, by our prayers and worship and consistent Christian life, we may help to bring that great day nearer. That day we must await with awe and godly fear, but also with faith and hope. Let us bear it in mind when we approach the altar of God, that there we are continuing a perpetual memory of his precious death until his coming again.

ADVENT 2

The Bible

Luke 4.21 *'Today in your very hearing this text has come true.'* (Jesus speaking in the temple when he reads Isaiah).

1 *The Literature*

Today is known as Bible Sunday. Let me begin by affirming positively to all who love language and literature that there is no comparison whatsoever with what the Bible contains. Of course, it is infinitely more for the Christian than language and literature of a high order; but let us start at this point. Everything and every day is raised to a noble height by the themes and subjects, with which this unique collection of books has to deal.

We may consider the almost classical introduction of St Luke's Gospel, often called the most beautiful book in the world, from which today's memorable scene of our Lord reading from Isaiah and then claiming to be the subject of the prophet's message is taken. We think of the opening chapter of the Letter to the Hebrews, and to the Colossians, the first chapter of St John, and—for sheer poetic beauty and theological thrust—1 Corinthians 13.

2 *The Themes*

(a) The Bible gives us a love *of history*. Across the pages names pass, Egypt, Babylon, Persia, Greece, Rome and little Israel, a Pharaoh here, a Cyrus and Nebuchadnezzar there. We are wise to take all history seriously. This, after all, is involved if we take our Lord's incarnation seriously.

(b) This library of books has stretched the mind with *great concepts* often too big for human comprehension: election; predestination; life and death; heaven and hell; Father, Son and Holy Spirit; time and eternity. Here are seers, prophets, priests and evangelists; the men of the desert—who went out into silence that they might come back with a word; a word that they had to speak, else they would die. They found it in the desert and preached it in town and village. We find ourselves stretched as we wrestle with these mighty concepts.

(c) The Bible introduces us to *great people*; Abraham striding out of the comforts and high civilisation of Ur, where they had central heating and worked at cube roots. Out he went at the call of God to found a nation to be the agent of his salvation. Moses guiding this people to the promised land, learning how small he was and how great God was. Out goes lonely Job marked by his great endurance, crying out against injustice, wrestling with his comforter. Out steps young Jeremiah crying out against God, who had deceived him—God's word like a fire in his bones. Out steps Hosea with a broken heart. Out of his tragedy came a gospel of a God with a broken heart who longed to bring back Israel, who had gone awhoring. Out steps a young village girl who dared to say, 'Behold the handmaid of the Lord', and who taught her son to pray. Out steps Peter, the expert at opening his mouth and putting his foot in it. Out steps Paul, the little Jew. You can meet him, so human, often almost subhuman, even almost superhuman, a man in Christ, traveller, correspondent, pastor, debtor to Jew and Gentile, the Jew writing a Greek interpretation of the good news of Jesus. He took the great central themes out of the rural language of Galilee and took them into the sophisticated language of the town and city.

(d) The Bible conveys to us *the Christ*. We see a sacramental principle at work. When you come to Communion the Holy Spirit does a miracle, takes ordinary things, bread, wine, the stuff of life, and through these things conveys the truth of the life of Christ. When a person or a group of people read the Bible, the Holy Spirit has a way of getting to work and conveying Christ through it to heart and mind. That is why Luther spoke of the Bible as the cradle that brings the cross to us. We do not worship the Bible; we worship the Christ, the God, the Three in One.

Application

As Christ looks out at us he may look at us with rebuke, as at Philip; or with disappointment, as at Peter; or with penetrating question, as with 'Saul, Saul'; or with imperious command, 'Come follow me.' But if, as he does so, I look back in adoration and commitment, I enter into life abundant; and that is why the Bible matters more than any other written document in the world.

ADVENT 3

The priesthood

> Matt. 11.10 *'Here is my herald, whom I send on ahead of you, and he will prepare your way before you.'*

1 *The Call*

The priest is often asked the question, 'When did you decide to be ordained?' When he replies, 'I don't really know,' many people may look somewhat disappointed, perhaps hoping that he would have said, 'I heard a voice calling me in the middle of the night.' It could be said that the priest hears a voice calling him to give his life to God in a particular way, but seldom does it come sensationally or dramatically; rather is it a voice that comes through persons, places and occasions—a voice which may start as a whisper, growing in intensity as the years pass, until finally it is heard loud and clear, as the bishop lays his hands upon one's head and says those irrevocable words, 'Take authority to be a priest of God.'

If you visit any theological college, it is surprising to hear how different are the ways in which this call from God comes. The students in any one college have come from many different backgrounds and occupations. In a recent such visit I met the son of a bus driver, of a butcher and of an insurance broker. Some had come straight from school or university; others from the world of commerce and industry. In the discussion after my talk it became clear that for only a very few had it been a matter of accepting a clear and unmistakable call with everything made easy. For the vast majority it had been an uphill struggle all the way. For a considerable proportion it had meant beginning with disapproving parents, who saw in the priesthood no financial security or hope of worldly success; and ending with personal doubts up to the last moment as to whether they were truly called or not. For some it had been a constant struggle to meet the academic requirements, whilst most candidates had at some time burnt themselves in the fires of doubt and unbelief.

Not all, who come forward, are finally ordained. Many fall by the way, either because they find the priestly life different from what they first supposed, or because they have fallen to the temptations of the world. Yet in each case one can see the riches of God's grace at work, selecting and testing each candidate for the office and work of a priest.

2 The Testing

It is, however, not sufficient for a man to say, 'God is calling me to be a priest.' The Church has the responsibility to examine and pronounce whether any one man is truly called by God. In the Church of England the bishop is advised by a central advisory body, which takes great care during the selection procedure to determine that the candidates they interview have the potential qualities of good priesthood. Each candidate must have a deep love of and devotion to the person of our Lord and his Church. The candidate must be interested in people; an interest that will grow into a love of souls. This does not mean that he must from the start necessarily be a good mixer or find everybody equally interesting. Provided that he wants to love them into a relationship with Christ, the rest will follow through his training and growth in the spiritual life.

Academic ability is a desirable asset, but by no means essential. The majority of priests ordained today have not been to university. No candidate need feel debarred from offering himself on financial grounds, as the Church makes grants available for those men unable to meet the cost of training, and a sizable portion of our parish apportionment each year goes for this purpose.

It seems to me important from time to time to talk about the vocation to the priesthood, for unless the ordinary parish church is providing men for the ministry, then we have little cause for complaint if the priests are not available when they are needed. I happen to have had the enormous privilege of seeing twenty-eight young men go forward from the parishes, where I have been priest, to the sacred ministry, but I reflect that I have also had at various times over thirty men as curates. The equation needs to be balanced in our minds.

3 The discipline

So far I have considered the material and machinery of making a priest. But above all this, the Christian priesthood is to make apparent to the world one all-consuming and explosive idea that man was made for the worship of God, and that only by faith in Jesus Christ may mankind find peace and true happiness. Everything in the priest's life must be subordinate to the propagation of these two ideas. He must be willing to undergo all kinds of problems, perhaps including poverty, persecution and loneliness, in the execution of his task. He knows that from the moment he decides to be a priest he places himself in the forefront of the struggle with the powers of darkness. He is a marked man; his slightest failing will be magnified.

Things, which are good and legitimate for his brother laymen, must often be rejected by the priest, if he sees them detracting from the fulfilment of his calling. For some there is the choice of remaining unmarried, because for them marriage would be an impediment in the way of their vocation. Their married brothers may, likewise, have to be prepared to forego the security of a settled existence, to see their children grow up and be educated in circumstances not wholly to their liking. Most learn to live without the luxuries which today the world regards as necessities for normal living. In all these things the humble crucified Christ must be their constant example.

In his struggle for the salvation of souls God has given the priest only two weapons of the spirit—the Word of God and the holy sacraments. At his ordination he is solemnly charged to expound and make known the will of God for man. This is a responsibility which weighs heavily upon his shoulders, for how shall they hear without a preacher? And it will be by these very words of God that each soul, committed to his care, will one day be judged before the throne of God. For this reason alone every careless Christian, every impenitent sinner, is a constant source of concern to the priest.

Many Christians would perhaps be surprised and become more faithful, if they realized just how much sorrow they caused their priest, when a familiar face was absent from the Communion rail on Sunday mornings; for equally at his ordination the priest is charged to be a faithful dispenser of Christ's holy sacraments. Herein lies the greatest privilege of the priest—to stand and act in the place of Christ at the holy table; to celebrate as the head of God's people the Holy Communion; to plead with Christ, that one and all-sufficient sacrifice of himself, to the Father; and then to feed his flock with the Body and Blood of their Saviour. There can be no greater work than this, building God's people into the ways of holiness. At the

26

heart of every problem which faces our world stands the individual with his actions and beliefs. Until each individual will is won and consecrated to our Lord, this world will never find the peace it longs for, and it is exactly at this invididual level that the priest does his work.

An appeal

As always, the Church cries out for more priests. If the Church is to perform her primary duty, I say to any young man, who may have listened so far, the Church may need you to question your vocation, whether you should be serving God as a layman—and God knows how much diligent Christian layment are needed! What he may also be saying to you is this, 'Is there a reason why you should not respond to the call to the sacred ministry?' If there is, God—not your own assessment of the situation—will show it you.

ADVENT 4

Following the Saviour

> Matt. 1.21 *'She will bear a son; and you shall give him the name Jesus (Saviour) for he will save his people from their sins.'*

1 *Jesus the Saviour*

All over the world an immense number of people will, in a day or two, be specially remembering the birth of a very great leader of men, whose memory is very fragrant. We remember that he was born of a good family in almost complete obscurity, that he grew up to attend his village school and to work in the family shop until he was in his late twenties. We remember that it was not till then that he came at all permanently before the public eye, and then only three brief years were to run before he was to die. As a child there was evidence of a strong will in at least one matter, which he believed of importance, but that strong will he continued to submit to the will of his parents for many years after he was old enough to live his own life.

In his short time as a great leader we find him apparently completely unmoved by the fact that for a period large crowds collected whenever he spoke in public. Afterwards, for a while his teaching was rather commonly despised, and for part of the time he was in hiding for his life. Not infrequently he had no place and no time to eat or sleep, and through all this, we are told of him, that he never asked of his followers any sacrifice or suffering which he did not share himself. Quite often, we learn, he spent the whole night in prayer while his men slept, sometimes walking about in the foothills and praying in the dark in the closest touch with heaven. Always he quietly and steadily kept his integrity; no reason, however plausible, ever made him by a hair's breadth lower his standards. He was the essence of tenderness and care for the sick; and even in the greatest stress of circumstances, as death came near to him and there was so much still to do, always there was time for all who through their own fault had made a mess of their lives and came to him for help in making a fresh start. With all his attention to personal cases went an opinion of great clarity upon questions of right and justice and the service of God. His pronouncements have never really been opposed or bettered, and his far-seeing vision saw the needs of men for many generations ahead and laid down the only system by which every nation could have security.

When he came to die, stripped naked in the middle of a hostile crowd in the midday sun outside an Eastern city, after having been betrayed by one of his own men, his main earthly concern was that his mother should be provided for and that no punishment should come upon those responsible for his death. So he died. This is the story of Lord Jesus. This is the story of him who is our Saviour. Many today, reading of him thus, might reasonably say, 'If such a man were living today, I'd follow him all the way.'

And if you find yourself whispering in your heart, 'Yes, I will go with him'; if that is your answer, then even if you have made the same answer before and afterwards have failed to come with him when things were difficult, he will not forsake you, he will teach you to do and suffer at least something of what he does and suffers, and he will give you the strength for this, as he did to his disciples, who ran away at first when he was arrested. For remember this, you are the agents of his salvation in the world.

It is important also to remember that we are not alone in our discipleship. As we begin to go with Jesus, we are immediately aware of an enormous multitude of people, who at some time or other have said that they also were going with him. Sometimes greater, sometimes less, sometimes carrying all before it, sometimes seeming to make no headway, this great army of persevering Christians has passed down the ages, as it is passing also in this age. It matters so much that this whole body of Christians should be alive and real, so that God's will may work through it, to bring to the world the salvation for which he came and to save men and women from their sins. As we kneel at Bethlehem, to follow Christ may seem easy, but when we rise to continue the journey, difficulties appear.

First, Christianity at one time became fashionable, and we have never quite become used to the fact that it is unfashionable now. That is to say that there is still a large number of professing Christians, who, while from time to time conforming to the outward customs and beliefs of some form of Christianity, actually in their lives bear very little resemblance to what even the outside world would expect one of Christ's companions to be.

Secondly, there are our personal failures—yours and mine. We do immense harm to the cause of our Lord, for this reason, that people judge him by what they see of us. Yet he came to save us from our sins.

Thirdly, is the continued hampering of the cause of Jesus Christ in the world by the divisions amongst his followers.

29

We must continue to pray about this. Division in the Church is a mark of sin. Jesus prayed that we might be one. Somewhere in his heart is the answer, and if we get near enough to him he will surely tell us.

SUNDAY AFTER CHRISTMAS DAY

Christian peace

Luke 2.29 *'Let your servant go in peace.'*

The traditional Christmas greeting about peace on earth and goodwill amongst men has been met during most of the years of the twentieth century with a good deal of cynicism and, maybe, with open derision. This is hardly to be wondered at when for so many of those years the world's affairs have been characterized by anything but goodwill, and when much of the peace seems to have been the uneasy peace of the truce variety. But we need to remind ourselves that it was in circumstances exceedingly like these that the original Christmas was set.

1 *Unpeaceful Bethlehem*

When Jesus was born in Bethlehem in Judaea in the days of Herod the king, the season was not conspicuous for either of the virtues of peace or goodwill, which are now associated with it. He was not born into a Christmas card view of holly and robins and well-behaved citizens going to church, but he was born into the Roman province of Palestine, racked by the remembrance of civil war, the expectation of revolt and the furious conflict of religious and political ideologies. Government was only held together forcibly in a precarious thirty years' peace by the unscrupulous old Herod, who, after a lifetime of political fence-sitting, was by this time dying on a usurped and bloodstained throne.

Nor could the inn itself have been filled with a particularly well-wishing and peaceful atmosphere, since it was crowded with people who had been ordered out of their homes and businesses to come and fill up income tax returns—conditions liable to produce irritation and temper at the best of times.

Our habitual way of keeping Christmas rather tends to push these realities out of sight, and so it encourages too many people to suppose that the peace and goodwill, which the Christ came to bring, were of an exterior kind. So today let us quite simply say some words about who *the* Christmas Day is all about and what he thought about the kind of peace that he came to bring. Statesmen's peace and Christ's peace have little to do with one another.

2 *Statesmen's peace*

Let us deal with statesmen's peace first. The strongest motive in any non-religious individual or community is self-interest. The self-interest of any two or more non-religious men or nations will obviously conflict very soon. So the statesmen aim at making some agreement which will be the best possible harmonizing of these conflicting claims of self-interest, and so achieve the greatest possible mutual good for the greatest numbers—at the same time leaving the various self-interests untouched at root. This delicate balance is called peace. The main point about it is that it is extremely precarious and so far has never stayed put for very long.

3 *Christian peace*

Christian peace is the opposite. Jesus' proposals for peace between neighbours and communities is to batter down self-interest in every one of us and finally to crush the life out of it altogether. He never remotely suggested that he would ever make any compromise with self-interest in anyone. On the contrary he said with emphasis: 'If any man would be my disciple, let him deny himself', that is—let him say 'no' to self—'and take up his cross and follow me.' There is no other interpretation of such remarks as: 'He who would lose his life for my sake will find it.' That is what the disconcerting babe of Bethlehem said and thought about the matter when he grew up, and if you do not like it or if you think it impracticable, then I suggest you cross his birthday off your calendar and go to work on Christmas Day rather than waste time on mass idealism.

THE SECOND SUNDAY AFTER CHRISTMAS

Lessons from the Epiphany

> Matthew 2.2 *'Where is the child who is born to be king of the Jews? We observed the rising of his star, and we have come to pay him homage.'*

1 *Christ the focus of attention*

To those of us who have been brought up as more catholic members of the Church of England, I suppose the Christmas crib holds a quite unique position. All over the world there are cribs, small and great, each with its own distinctive beauty. We have most of us worshipped in churches where, from cheap and simple materials, from straw and brown paper and Christmas tree frost and a couple of old packing cases, a crib has been made, often very beautifully. We have also seen costly and expensive cribs with figures of great intrinsic beauty and worth, such as those to be seen in many of our great cathedrals and major parish churches. But always the keynote of the crib is simplicity, matched by the simple people present—a shepherd or two picked up at random from the fields, and a carpenter, who has been refused a night's lodging, and his wife and her baby. Anybody, who wanted models for a set of crib figures, could find them in the nearest social services centre.

A disturbance

And then comes the Feast of the Epiphany, and we come to Church to find there has been a disturbance and rearrangement in that familiar group under the stable eaves. There are sometimes camels and elephants, outlandish beasts to us. There is a negro, bringing a foreign note into the picture. There are expensive-looking gifts lying on the edge of the straw.

Whatever the disturbance, however, and whatever the rearrangement, the Christ child is always central, always the focus of attention.

2. *Power consecrated to Christ*

There can be no disputing the supremacy of natural science over the thought and daily life of men and women. What is less certain is the benefit it confers in hard terms on human happiness. Once it was thought that the reign of science must inaugurate an era of peace and plenty, of sanity and mutual understanding. How sadly we have been disillusioned! We know today that it produces a variety of heightened tensions and ever more frightful disasters, and many ask, can they lead to the culmination of annihilation of civilisation?

The only answer to this fearful dilemma depends upon the attention which the world gives to the lesson of the Epiphany—the showing of the infant Christ to the whole world. The Magi, or wise men, were scientists, skilled in the lore of their day and particularly in astronomy. As used by them, however, it was not an imperious master leading its servants to destruction. On the contrary, it guided them to the fuller revelation of God and to the feet of the infant Christ.

The Magi were kings, too. They were men of power in their own countries, and we live in an age of power as well as of science and technology. The doctrine of naked power was never preached so unashamedly as in this century, and was never accepted without question over so large a portion of the globe. Dictators of past ages were never armed with such overwhelming power as present-day governments. The very achievements of technology have placed unparalleled resources of power in the hands of the central authorities of the state.

The Epiphany is a parable of the consecration of power. Three kings came in their splendour and laid their offerings at the feet of a mightier king. The amazing thing is that this king, whose sovereignty they acknowledged, is a newborn babe, the son of Mary. By their obeisance they confessed that the earthly ruler, however powerful, has a supreme overlord, a master whose authority does not depend upon brute force, but upon the intrinsic claims of law, justice, morality and love. They are conscious, quite simply, of their stewardship. When I was confirmed, the good priest who prepared me wrote in the flyleaf of the Confirmation manual, which he gave me, the words from St Paul's First Letter to the Corinthians: 'It is required in stewards that a man be found faithful.'

3 *Unity focussed in Christ*

This age is again one that searches desperately for unity. Never were the disasters, which are attendant upon disunity, so obvious or so formidable; and the abiding message of Epiphany is one of unity. The kings, who followed the star, represent different creeds and needs. Yet, as they kneel before the crib, they are united. The humble shepherds join with them, the workers of the earth with the rulers of the earth, and the dumb creatures add their presence. All are united by a fellowship in worship. Before the babe in a manger, this King of kings and Lord of lords, differences fall away and they are at one with each other. Tell me, if you can imagine a more exalted conception!

It is in this way alone that unity comes to man. As between nations, it comes about when the rulers and parliaments of different countries freely acknowledge the authority of divine law and confess that the justice of God is more important than national self-interest. As between classes, it springs from the recognition that God's love is bestowed freely on all men in creation and in redemption; and of this the incarnation is a token. As between members of one family, it comes when this group is made the centre of the home and the infant Saviour adored by all. The only unity that is real and permanent is the result of humble submission to the babe of Bethlehem and the determination to obey his will for the Church and for the world.

Conclusion

Where is the child? Where indeed in our modern power-craving, fragmented world? Where is the Christ child in whose homage alone power is safe and unity realized? Christmas shows him once again to us. Will we make him the focus of our lives?

EPIPHANY 1

The Work of the Spirit

John 1.32 'I saw the Spirit coming down from heaven like a dove and resting upon him.'

'God is a hesitant hit, but the Church a decided miss' was the summation of a debate by some young people recently on the present religious situation in England. Most would probably agree. There is still a widespread readiness to believe in God; a genuine respect for the person of Jesus; but a doubt about the institutional Church as a valid bearer of the Christian Gospel. England is no longer a Christian nation in any meaningful sense. The old landmarks have gone; the old forms of mission which served so well in their time are now outdated, and we have to discover the patterns which God wants us to use today. The Church is now out in the open, stripped of its power and privilege. It is seen as a decreasing minority.

1 *Blazing the future trail*

In this situation, how can the mission be carried forward? What are the forms of mission most suitable today? As always, the Holy Spirit has gone ahead to prepare the way for us, and it is possible to see movements of the spirit blazing the future trail. During the past twenty years many parishes have discovered the value of house-churches, where small groups of Christians gather in a home for bible study and prayer, to plan for evangelism and often to Break Bread. Similar groups have, of course, become familiar in factories, business houses, hospitals and schools. These often have the advantage of being ecumenical.

In another way, the Holy Spirit has been active in the calling into being of new types of Christian community, such as Lee Abbey and St Julian's, Scargill, in our own Church; the Little Brothers of Jesus and Foccolari, within the Roman Catholic tradition; and, strikingly, the compelling magnetism of the voice of reconciliation expressed at Taizé, where the eighty resident brothers represent thirty denominations.

These groups are no new thing in the life of the Church, and indeed represent a return to earlier forms of mission which have never completely died out. The Church was rooted in the homes of people for several centuries before there were church buildings. It is, therefore, a serious question to ask ourselves whether our buildings are a help or a hindrance to the spread of the Gospel today. The influence of the small informal group far beyond its numbers was evident, too, in the work of the friars in the Middle Ages, among eighteenth century Evangelicals and in the Clapham Sect of the last century. The history of the Christian Church provides ample evidence that the Spirit speaks more often than not to groups rather than to a whole institution or to isolated individuals.

For centuries the Church has been dominated by the clergy, and this idea dies hard. There are far too many lay people who are not only content to leave all the work to the parsons, but sincerely believe that they are paid for it and, therefore, it is their job. There are also still too many parsons who believe that the laity should be passive and obedient. There are certainly dangers in the voluntary principle, for groups may become independent of the mainstream of church life, and sectarian; they may become isolationist and divisive; they may become escapist from the issues of life, and holy huddles sheltering from the pressures of the world. But they can become bridge-builders; they can penetrate the life of society; they can give room for that flexibility and lay initiative, of which we often speak but see so little. Far better to run the risks than to find ourselves in a groove of yesterday that rapidly becomes a grave for tomorrow.

2 Challenging the place of structures

Above all, the voluntary principle of the informed group is vital because it reflects a right doctrine of the Holy Spirit. If one thing is true of the Holy Spirit, it is that he cannot be bound and structured. There is a real danger in the Church today of over-centralization and of its becoming a vast machine. The spontaneous group can better meet the needs of a highly mobile and changing society than mono-lithic organizations. For mission today we need structures which are informal and temporary, which can easily be broken up when a particular job is done; and which are able to experiment boldly without fear of being bound by past traditions. The Spirit is a spirit of freedom. The Spirit of Jesus must always be a spirit of protest against the estab-lished order—where that is seen to be defective. It may well be that this Spirit is more easily reflected through the living organism of the group than through the institutional church, which of necessity is a more cumbrous organisation. It is dangerous and wrong to set the informal group over against the formal structure—both are needed and both constitute the Church as the bearer of the Gospel. We do well to ask ourselves whether our local church is bound to the patterns of the past (usually of Victorian or Edwardian days), or open to respond to the Holy Spirit. How deeply do we know our fellow church members; how open are we to one another?

3 *Reshaping methods of evangelism*

Without question, the gap between Christian and non-Christian grows steadily wider as society becomes more secular, more violent, more materialistic, more greedy. The task of evangelism becomes harder and its process longer. More and more do some thinking Christians question the methods of the mass crusade—typified by the ministry of such outstanding evangelists as Dr Billy Graham. This is certainly not to scorn the work of such great men, or to doubt the new life in Christ which many have found through their ministry. It is, however, to put some honest question marks over using that approach today. Evangelism through fellowship has been found to speak to many today. When a reclaimed Moonie recently said to me: '*I did not really believe their jargon; but at a time of a broken home and a lost job they said: "Let us love you and guide you through your problems",*' I saw in this a great indictment of the institutional church, for Christianity must be seen to be a community rather than a code. Lee Abbey and Scargill and other such centres have found time and again that our Lord speaks not only through the words of individuals, in epilogues and study groups, but much more through the impact of the fellowship of the Holy Spirit expressed in and through the shared life of the communities living there.

Has this something intensely relevant to say about our approach to the vast unchurched masses in our great cities today?

EPIPHANY 2

The Friendship of Christ

John 1.39 *They went and saw where he was staying, and spent the rest of the day with him.*

How extraordinary to see where Jesus of Nazareth was living! To see where he had his meals; to see where he slept! How extraordinary to be asked to spend the day with him! It was like staying with a friend. But that is what he actually called his disciples. 'I call you servants no longer', he said, 'I call you friends.'

Religion has as its purpose and aim the drawing of the human soul into ever closer touch with God. Our faith is the means by which we may be brought into touch with God. It is the link by which the human soul is brought into an abiding friendship with God. There is no nobler name than that of friend; to be a friend is to be admitted into relationship and co-operation. It is to be loved and to be understood and persuaded, but never to be forced. It is to share in another's joys and burdens and secret thoughts, so that our very mind and spirit can be one with that of another. Friendship is the doorway into all the best things in life. We come to see with others' eyes things to which we had previously been blind. This, humanly speaking, accounts in some measure for the hidden powers of those who really know Christ. He says to us today, as he said to his first disciples, 'I call you not slaves, but friends.' There is a world of difference between being a servant and being a friend.

1 *Christ's friendship does not dominate*

Christ could have commanded his disciples. He could have dominated them. He could have bidden them to believe this or that without question. Why did he not give them a creed and so save all the great conflicts of early Christendom? He might have dictated their every action and they

39

would have obeyed him. Why did he not turn his teaching into a book of regulations? It would have been easier for all of us. Most of us have something in us which longs for this kind of control, but it was not his way. When people wanted explicit guidance he would throw them back to the voice within: 'What do you think yourself?' There are no rules in the teaching of Jesus except the command to love. What Jesus did was to admit people to his friendship. He gave himself to them, sharing with them his thoughts about life and money and God, but only as they were willing to trust him fully and to learn. Our Lord never stood to dictate or to coerce, and what agony it must sometimes have caused him! Think of his letting Judas go, when one sudden strong note of appeal might have brought him to his knees, but the Son of God refused to dominate.

This distinction is the key to all right relations between us and others, between parents and children, husbands and wives, masters and men. Many a so-called friendship breaks down because on the part of one there is a subtle desire to dominate. We like sometimes to try to form the opinion of others, to dictate to them their conduct. What we call love may be corrupted by this desire for power, and our affection for the other may become only the satisfaction of unconscious pride. Because of this, strain sometimes breaks out between parents and children. We may seek to dominate our children, to coerce them, to try to make them into the image of ourselves or, more often, of what we have not been able to become. 'What she called love', says a writer of a mother in one of his books, 'was only her enjoyment of her son's leaning upon her.' He was a slave and not a friend. Is not this distinction also the key to the agelong conflict between employers and employees? Peace never really comes into industry until this demand for a real partnership is understood.

2 Christ's friendship conveys power

Christ's friendship had in it, and still has, a far surer power.

Through his love truth became clear; the way of right became obvious; conscience was clear. The whole world of goodness and love became alive through him, and in the obedience that followed they were free, because they were taking the road of their surrender through desire. Life became a glad companionship, in which they walked with him in the kind of bondage which they willingly followed. They were not servants; they were friends.

There are no other terms on which we can know the secret of Christian living. In no other way can we become really free from the power of evil. He wins us out of it if we allow him to do so, and, as we come to know him as friend, wrong things become impossible because we ceased to want to do them. He will not compel us out of sin except by that love of him, which expels it from the heart. We sometimes wish he would. We would like God to save us in spite of our resistance. If he could, it would be to exchange one form of servitude for another. We would not be friends; we would be slaves.

Application

So there is but one way into real freedom, to let his love so fill our minds that it takes possession of our souls. It is to come to know him so that he can become our friend; and deep in our hearts we long for that possession by him. A recent writer has said: 'I sometimes think that the love of God can only be a reality to the very lonely; to others he is merely a theory or an idea.' But which of us at heart is not lonely? There are rooms that human love can only partially fill. We need the perfect friend, perfect in understanding and in rebuking and forgiving. He holds out his hand. He offers his friendship. The lonely burden becomes one that we share with him; but it all depends on how far we allow the Son of God to enter.

41

EPIPHANY 3

Medicine for Depression

> John 6.12 'Collect the pieces left over, so that nothing may be lost.'

1 Depression

Every parish priest nowadays must be constantly aware in his visiting that a considerable number of his people are depressed. He will know, too, that the depression arises from the fact that people feel a loss of a sense of security. After all, the great wars of this century and the difficulties of arriving at any subsequent agreement have cast over the minds of all thoughtful people the shadow of the possibility of yet another world conflict, and with it the horror of the latest methods of destruction. There cannot very often have been a time, when our Lord's teaching against over-anxiety for the things of the morrow, and his call to live in simple trust upon God as each day dawns, needed more to be taken to heart. A young mother, whose husband had been taken from her by the calls of military service and who was having a difficult and lonely struggle, said to me recently that her fears were not the result of any serious personal trouble, but that things in general made her feel 'just fed-up'.

Here is one of those phrases which describes exactly the mental despair which sours everything and takes all the joy out of life. In these difficult days we most of us know the mood only too well—when everybody seems to be in a conspiracy to annoy us and without any definite reason, our whole outlook is shadowed with gloom and life simply does not seem worth living.

2 Accidie

But this is not a new thing. The mediaeval moralists had a name for this temper of mind which is equally subtle and forceful. They called it *accidie* and regarded it as one of the deadly sins. The preachers of the time had a good deal to say about it, and it is given a dreadful doom in Dante's *Inferno*. It was very prevalent in the monasteries. Cassian, one of the founders of western monasticism, defined *accidie* as 'a disgust of soul or weariness of life'. Here is what this old writer says: 'When a monk is first attacked by it, he detests his cell. He becomes critical and thinks that his brother monks are unspiritual and neglectful of their duties. He dwells much on the excellence of other and distant monasteries, and the more distant they are the more excellent he thinks them. He pictures to himself the pleasant and profitable life there, whereas all that immediately surrounds him is harsh and distasteful.'

Accidie is the characteristic temper of our time. The whole world is a depressed area, and it is a very superficial mistake to suppose that the depression is merely an economic one. Behind national and international discord there is a psychological depression, a wellnigh universal feeling of discontent and disillusionment, which destroys confidence. One of the most pathetic results of war is a wreckage of hope; and following great wars there is a negative attitude towards thought and art and literature, expressing a sense of the meaningless and futility of life.

3 *Six pieces of advice*

How then can this depression be overcome? As it is not a positive difficulty, it is not easy to face up to it and grapple with it. As a rule, we would be hard put to it to say why we get so depressed, and it is precisely this vagueness which makes depression so difficult to deal with. While there is no infallible specific, which will meet the needs of every case and every temperament, there are some well-tried remedies which are of great help to us in our hours of discouragement, and, if employed regularly, in the majority of cases effect a cure.

First, one's health plays a big part. Our bodies and minds and souls are not separate and detached. We live a complete, rounded life, in which one part of our complex nature profoundly influences another, and a low-tone condition of mental and spiritual life may be due to a low-tone condition of physical life.

Secondly, we must realize that depression is a sin. We are much too apt to make excuses for it, to put the blame on ill-health or temperament or trouble of one kind or another, and to treat it as something which is quite outside the control of the will. Though troubles and difficulties will sorely tax the faith of the bravest in most lives, they need not and ought not to overcome them. We can check and thwart, by self-mastery, both a constant tendency to depression and the many circumstances tempting us to give way, just as we can give free course to it by weakness and self-indulgence. To say that we cannot get the better of our moods is to contradict universal and everyday experience and to deny the power of grace to discipline and strengthen the will.

Thirdly, we must avoid talking about depressing things. Psychology has taught us a great deal about autosuggestion, the process whereby through means of our conscious mind an idea is implanted on our unconscious mind and left to develop there. It seems to be generally agreed that the spoken word is a powerful factor in autosuggestion and our mental outlook is influenced profoundly, though unconsciously, by the things we talk about. There are not a few people who seem to take a ghoulish delight in talking about misfortune and illnesses; accidents, bereavements and troubles of one kind or another form their conversational stock-in-trade. Every clergyman knows the time spent listening to the intricate details of surgical operations. But remember that such talk has its powerful mental reactions, both upon ourselves and upon others. When you are depressed, try hard not to talk about your despondency. Avoid expressing the matter outwardly at all, if you can help it.

Fourthly, we must fight against self-absorption. In the last analysis all the causes of depression may be reduced to one—self-centredness. We get low-spirited because we think too much about ourselves, *our* health, *our* spiritual state, *our* circumstances, *our* troubles. If, when we are depressed, we project our thoughts away from ourselves and try to sympathize with and help someone who is in need, we shall find that the hole, out of which we pull our neighbour, will be the grave, in which we bury our own gloom. The saintly John Keble said, 'When you feel yourself overpowered, the best way is to go out and do something kind to someone or other.' One might almost make the motto for those who suffer very low spirits, 'Look up and not down; look forward and not back; look out and not in; and lend a hand.'

Fifthly, we have to cultivate a spirit of thankfulness. We are exceptional people indeed if our blessings do not far outnumber our discouragements. We matter. The thankful remembrance of all God's mercies to us will shame our faithlessness and encourage us to trust that the dark hour, through which we pass, is not the twilight after sunset but the twilight before the dawn.

Finally, we must always remember the blessed power that comes through prayer. Nothing can compare with prayer as a cure for low spirits, because prayer links us with him who said, 'Ask and you will receive, that your joy may be complete.' 'Come unto me, all that are weary and heavy-laden, and I will refresh you.'

At a meeting of the British Medical Association some years ago Dr Hyslop, Superintendent of the Bethlehem Hospital for Mental Diseases, said a striking thing in this connection. Here are his words, 'As one, whose life has been concerned with the suffering of the mind, I give it as my experience that of all the hygienic measures to counteract disturbed sleep, depressed spirits and all the miserable results of a mind diseased, I would undoubtedly give first place to prayer. Let there be a habit of nightly communion with God, not as a mere mendicant or repeater of the words of others, but as an individual who submerges his personality in the greater whole. Such a habit will do more to cleanse the mind and strengthen the soul than any other therapeutic agent known to man.' Words from such a source, spoken on such an occasion, come to us with an authority all their own. Prayer is an inexpensive medicine and for that reason it is often despised, but it is not an easy medicine to take. It requires a strong faith and a disciplined will. Yet, when so taken, it never fails. No troubles, even the greatest, can crush and dispirit us, if only we seek our strength from God in the sure confidence that 'underneath are the everlasting arms', and that he will guide and keep us through all the trials and difficulties of our earthly journey, 'till the day break and the shadows flee away'.

EPIPHANY 4

Distinctive church life

John 4.24 *'God is spirit, and those who worship him must worship in spirit and truth.'*

Not long ago I had the privilege of being included in a luncheon party for seven men in the central London office of a major industrial concern; the party included some managing directors, a leading actuary and a senior director of the Bank of England. We talked a lot about the technical and moral problems facing our nation and the world and, as is so often the case in such company, we talked about God.

1 *Distinctive buildings*

We had previously looked out from the window of this office suite in Queen Anne's Gate across St James's Park in one direction and over to Westminster Abbey in another. The Abbey that day had huge queues waiting to visit it; so we looked at a Gothic building holding its own amongst massive blocks of offices and shops, a structure quite unlike those which flanked it. The same is, of course, true of St Paul's Cathedral and other great and small places of worship.

Of course, the Church's life is not rooted in its buildings; the clergy are not ordained to be curators of attractive museums. The Church—that is the people who form the Church—hold a distinctive belief about existence. This belief is that God comes first and everything derives from him. The Church's distinctiveness is summed up in one of the truly definitive verses of the Book of the Acts—2.42: 'They met constantly to hear the apostles teach, and to share the common life, to break bread, and to pray.' Churches, therefore, should appear different simply because they proclaim something different. They proclaim, 'We believe in the natural and we also believe in the spiritual', and those are not contradictory. God is spirit, as our Lord said, but the spirit is proclaimed through those who value it in their lifestyle.

2 Distinctive life—four marks

Let us look a little closer at this distinctive life which marked out the infant Church. Its members met constantly. There circulates from time to time the argument that a man may be a Christian without going to church. Let us never forget that man derived his Christianity in the first place from the Church, even if indirectly. So the woman in today's story said to our Lord, 'You Jews say that the temple where God should be worshipped is in Jerusalem.' Without the Church the Christian Gospel and the Christian way of life would not have been preserved to this day. Christians, by meeting together, take action to see that our faith will be transmitted to future generations; gathering together makes for continuity.

(a) Teaching
But why did those early Christians meet constantly? Four reasons are given. They met in order to hear the apostles teach. Do not forget that Christ's followers are called first of all Christ's disciples and that word means 'learners'. We are learners about living the Christian way. The twelve apostles were twelve disciples before they became twelve

apostles. They were required to learn before they were sent out (the word 'apostle' means 'sent-out man'). Christian service is right, but not at the expense of meeting together constantly to hear Christian teaching; otherwise, the salt soon loses its savour.

(b) Sharing

Secondly, the early Church met in order to share the common life. It would be unthinkable in New Testament times for a Christian not to attend church and not be known, and not want to be known. The situation would be as grotesque as having a secret member of a family, someone who slipped into meals and slipped out again, without any sharing of the family's life or responsibility. There must be togetherness in a Church—a congregation, not just an aggregation. This togetherness is sustained when we recognize each other as fellow disciples in the same classroom.

(c) Hospitality

Thirdly, the early Christians broke bread together. What exactly this means in its historical setting is not clear. It could be a reference to a communal meal, of which the Eucharist originally formed a part, but the lesson is quite plain. We build up the distinctive life of the Church when we are hospitable, and we build it up when we make a point of meeting together to break bread in the Holy Communion. This is utterly distinctive of the Church's life and, indeed, is carrying on our Lord's explicit command.

(d) Praying

Fourthly, the early Christians met constantly to pray. To pray is not easy, but the Church is giving its finest witness when it prays, because it is underlining its belief in a power outside nature and outside man. The Church that does not pray becomes in the end a Church that does not exist. Faith without prayer is dead.

This then was the distinctive life that the people of Jerusalem saw spring up in their midst, with the coming of the Christian Church on the day of Pentecost. In the passage we have read today this whole achievement is foretold in the words of Jesus. 'It is from the Jews', he says, 'that salvation comes. But the time approaches when those who are real worshippers will worship the Father in spirit and in truth. Such are the worshippers whom the Father wants.' Well may we ask ourselves as members of today's Christian family, 'Are the people of Britain aware of any distinctive life which catches their attention?' There would be far less hope of this if all church buildings were demolished, and very little hope if Christians did not break bread and pray. Churchgoing is still vastly important, and private belief must be twinned to public witness, even before it is exemplified in public action.

EPIPHANY 5

The wisdom of God

> Matthew 12.42 *'The Queen of the South came from the ends of the earth to hear the wisdom of Solomon; and what is here is greater than Solomon.'*

How well I can remember during my eight years as a choirboy that the doubtless devout theological knowledge, delivered from the pulpit with such regularity, was painfully lost, so far at least as one treble chorister was concerned! Spiritual truth, though profound, I have come to believe since, is simple enough to be expressed in words understandable to the child; but often enough, in the way it is presented, there is very little that any young person, or indeed older ones, can grasp.

1 *What is God like?*

I am sure that today, despite the mass of evils that have been loosed in the world, the characteristic religious question is not, 'Is there a God?', as it was in the last century amongst a people influenced by Darwin and Huxley. Today men ask, 'What is God like?' and there are very few theorists among us. Here, then, is an apparently simple question that goes right to the root of our religion. In one sense we cannot picture God at all, because 'God is spirit and no man has seen God at any time.' Yet it is of supreme importance to know something of his nature and purpose, for it is our conception of God that shapes and colours our whole view of this universe and our own place in it.

So often people have wrong ideas about God. Some, for example, believe in *a tyrannical God*, arbitrary and capricious in his dealings, impatient with human weakness and folly, quick to punish any disobedience to his will, stern and hard like a great cosmic policeman. No wonder men turn away from such a God. Others believe in *an unjust God*. People often say to me, as I am sure to every priest, 'There is no justice in the world. Why should I have to suffer like this? I have always tried to live a good life. Why are the good punished, while the bad ones go on their way unrepentant and prosperous?' If that were to be true, small wonder that men would turn from a God like that. Others cannot believe in *an indifferent God*. He is far away, they think, not interested in the affairs of this little planet we call the earth, caring nothing for the struggles and aspirations, the sufferings and the fears of humanity.

2 *God is like Christ*

And so, perhaps the most important question in the whole universe of thought is, 'What is God like?' In answer to that question Christianity says, 'God is like Jesus Christ.' Let us finish the quotation made earlier, 'No man has seen God at any time. The only begotten Son, who is in the bosom of the Father, he has declared him.' That is to say,

50

Jesus came to reveal God, to give us a glimpse of the very heart of God. Consider for a moment the books we call the Gospels. They contain the story of the most beautiful life and character ever seen on our troubled earth. The Gospel writers painted, each in his own way, the picture of one who came to us from the eternal world into this world of time to dwell among men. See our Lord as he moves about the country roads and villages of Galilee; see him bending over the sick, laying his healing hand upon a leper, comforting the poor and the sad, stopping to talk to a tramp on the highway, offering forgiveness to those who have sinned and are sorry about it, stretching out a hand to those who have fallen in the dust, lifting them up again to new hope, and at last, hanging upon a cross in agony; and, even as he hangs there, praying for his enemies and, most marvellous of all, conquering pain, hatred and death itself, and coming back to his friends serene and triumphant from the grave. Across that whole life there is clearly written one word, 'love'—divine, victorious love. Now Christianity says that God is like our Lord, and if you look at Jesus you are looking into the very heart of Almighty God. Christ said that himself. He said, 'He that has seen me has seen the Father.' If, then, Jesus does in fact reveal God there is only one possible conclusion. God is love.

3 *The difficulty of beliving in a God of love*

Many people find this hard to believe. They look at the suffering and evil in the world. 'How can God be love, so long as war is allowed to go on?', they ask. Or they see sickness—strong men struck down by fever, women dying in childbirth, thousands tortured by the cruel pains of cancer, hospital wards crowded with sufferers. 'How can God be love, so long as there is pain in the world?' These are big questions and, indeed, there is no complete answer. For our finite minds the problem of evil will always hold something of baffling mystery at the heart of it. But two things may be said.

First, that the great mass of suffering in the world is not

51

due to the injustice of God but to the selfishness and stupidity, the greed and lust and evil of us men and women. Don't let us dare to make God responsible for our own sins! I think, if we are honest and impartial in our outlook upon the world, we shall have to admit that almost all those things which most tragically mar human life and spoil human salvation are, directly or indirectly, the result of human wrongdoing.

In the second place, Christianity proclaims that, in spite of appearances, God *does* care. He is not far off, unnoticing and aloof. On the contrary, he is our unseen Father, regarding us as his children; he made us; he understands us; he watches over us; he feels with us; he suffers with us; he numbers the hairs of our heads; he is near to us every hour from the day of our birth to the day of our death. There is a verse of a hymn I first sang in Sunday School, and which has remained with me all my life:

There is no place where earth's sorrows are more felt
    than up in heaven;
There is no place where earth's failings have such kindly
    judgement given;
For the love of God is broader than the measures of
    man's mind
And the heart of the Eternal is most wonderfully kind.

4 *The wisdom of God*

What then is the wisdom of God? It is contained in the famous words in St John's Gospel—'God so loved the world that he gave his only begotten Son that, whoever believes in him, should not perish but have everlasting life.' Christ is in himself the embodiment of God: wisdom. God did not set this planet of ours spinning upon its blind way through space and then leave its inhabitants alone to a chance destiny. On the contrary, he sent his own Son to this poor earth to enter into our human lot, to live in a workman's cottage, to toil with his hands, to rejoice and weep, to labour and suffer with ordinary men and women. As St John says, 'He lived with us and we saw his glory, the glory as of the only begotten of the Father, full of grace and truth.' This is the wisdom of God, a wisdom far, far greater than that of Solomon.

One other point. Many people in our time are living without God, restless, unsatisfied, longing to find peace of mind, asking sometimes in the depths of their souls, 'How can I know God? How can I become sure of his love and goodness?' The way is not by human wisdom, not by reasoning and debating and arguing; not by philosophy and the reading of many learned books; not, at least primarily, through the intellect at all. Men have seldom found God at the end of an argument. The more sure way is to open the heart to the wisdom of God, who is Jesus Christ our Lord. In him we see what God is like—a God of infinite love.

Application

If you are confused about things or lost in the dark wilderness of doubt or have wandered from the proper path, then you may do something very simple—so simple that we sometimes forget its efficacy. Kneel down very humbly on your knees and let all the haunting, clamouring voices of doubt die down in your heart and say quite simply, 'Our Father who art in heaven . . .'; and as surely as the dawn breaks when the night is over, the Father in heaven will hear your prayer and you will feel about you the light of his comforting presence; you will be in touch with the very wisdom of God.

EPIPHANY 6

Bold proclamation

Matthew 13.27 (JB) *'Sir, was it not good seed that you sowed in your field? If so where does the darnel come from?'*

There is a story of the taciturn President Hoover that, when asked on returning from a Church service what the sermon had been about, he replied briefly, 'Sin'. Being further pressed as to what the preacher had said about it, he replied, 'He was against it'.

1 *Clear teaching on vice and virtue*

It is surely an odd state of affairs when it is thought necessary to ask a Christian priest to state publicly that the Christian religion is against vice and favours virtue. But that was precisely what several letters, written to me following my New Year's message about materialism to a local newspaper, suggested that I did. The writers suggested that a clear restatement in this respect by the Church's leaders was needed. Public memories are short, and it is worth remembering the number of unspectacular and regular ways in which the Christian Churches are continually bearing witness to light against darkness, and all that is sick and neurotic and evil, in favour of whatsoever things are pure and lovely and of good report.

Thousands of children in Church day and Sunday schools and in Confirmation classes are regularly brought face to face with the ten commandments and our Lord's summary of the law. Half the marriages in this country still take place in church, with all the opportunities for careful instruction, which most clergy are eager to use. Church societies work in ceaseless compassion for those who are having to bear the consequences of ignorance, weakness or lust. Industrial chaplaincies bear witness that God's law covers social as well as personal behaviour; and very much more besides is incorporated into the Church's witness to the law and the love of God.

2 *Progress and regression*

Human nature is fairly constant. In some ways our generation is more moral than our forbears. Concern for economic and racial equality and hatred of war and poverty have rarely been stronger. In other ways we are regressing. Violence is more readily accepted, perhaps more than at any time since the eighteenth century. There was plenty about before that.

In sexual ethics we are reverting to paganism. The social acceptance of abortion and the public performance of sexual intercourse were characteristic of the Roman Empire at its time of decadence. For many, obsession with sex makes the whole thing a big bore. But two features are new. First, the mass media makes available to all what used to be features of an élite. The coarseness of the eighteenth century caricaturists, for example, was popular, but *Private Eye* has more resources. Beardsley could not show his drawings on television; Restoration comedy had not the scope of an 'X' certificate. Secondly, widespread methods of contraception have given to women a sexual liberty, which no previous generation has known. Whether the double standard was good or bad, it has gone.

3 *A missionary situation*

For some time now we have been saying that England is in a missionary situation, so it should not surprise us that the features which characterized the Corinth or the Rome to which St Paul wrote his Letters, are again to be seen. Now, as then, the call to the Church is to proclaim the judgment and the mercy of God. It is a call to extol the new life in Christ, but it is a call, above all, to exhibit it in a Christian community which out-lives, out-thinks and out-loves the surrounding society. In our Gospel today, the owner of his field instructed the servants to let both the good seed and the weeds (called 'darnel' in the Jerusalem Bible) grow together until the harvest, when at that time the sorting out would take place. It is during this growing period that the Christian community is called to show, by its loving and caring, just how much our way of life means to us.

'Praise be to the God and Father of our Lord Jesus Christ, who in his great mercy gave us new birth into a living hope by the resurrection of Jesus Christ from the dead!' (1 Peter 1.3)

'He rescued us from the domain of darkness and brought us away into the kingdom of his dear Son, in whom our release is secured and our sins forgiven' (Colossians 1.13)

NINTH SUNDAY BEFORE EASTER

Time and talents

Luke 8.15: '*The seed in good soil represents those who bring a good and honest heart to the hearing of the word, hold it fast, and by their perseverance yield a harvest.*'

1 *Redeeming our time*

I suppose many of us, especially as we get older, remember clichés about parents and grandparents. My grandmother used to say repeatedly, 'Each day we take one step nearer home'—not exactly easily comprehended by a little boy! When I was in the diocese of Chester, and therefore, frequently visited that remarkable cathedral, there was a favourite and famous inscription I read there, which reads:

'When I was a child I laughed and wept—time crept;
When I was a youth I waxed more bold—time strolled;
When I became a full-grown man—time ran;
When older still I daily grew—time flew;

56

Soon I shall find in passing on—time gone.
O Christ, wilt thou have saved me then? Amen'

Like so many poems about time that little poem gives us a
feeling of urgency. It is a feeling put another way in
Psalm 90:

'For in thy sight a thousand years are as yesterday;
a night-watch passes, and thou hast cut them off;
they are like a dream at daybreak,
they fade like grass which springs up with the morning
but when evening comes is parched and withered.'

The whole of that psalm is a most wonderful reflection on
life, which is why it is often used at a funeral service. It
certainly repays careful study by Christians.

The urgency, which these sayings give us, is not the
kind that prompts us to rush around. It is an urgency
which reminds us that there are some really important
things to do in life before it is too late. Often our Lord
reminds us, as he does in today's parable, that it is for us to
use our stewardship of all that God has given us with a
deep sense of proper urgency, which he links to perseverance; indeed, today he says: 'by their perseverance they
will yield a harvest.'

We often put off doing something important, only to
discover that it is too late to remedy it. We mean to write a
letter or to visit when a friend is ill; before we have done it,
the person dies. Many early Christians had a great sense of
urgency; they believed that time was running out on them.
One of our well-known modern hymns reflects that sense:

'Redeem thy mis-spent time that's past,
Live this day as if t'were thy last.'

2 Using our talents

In other words, time is not on our side; therefore use the
talents that God has given you. Every so often we hear
about some new infant prodigy. It is well-known that
Mozart could compose from the age of four. In the

borough in which I live, I often come across children who are highly gifted in music and other spheres. In fact, when we hear the expression, 'a gifted child', we usually think of one with an exceptional talent; but it cannot be said too often that everyone of us is gifted. A favourite bygone phrase was, 'I took my harp to a party but no one asked me to play'. It is a phrase underlining the fact that here was someone with a modest talent and nobody wanted to know. Probably next time he didn't bother to take his harp. Whilst we may not be able to play the harp, we all have talents, however modest.

The urgent need to use our gifts is all the more important when we look at our Christian ministry. 'Whatever can *I* do?' is all too often the feeling of the man and woman in the pew. There seems to be an assumption that only the clergy have gifts of ministry. Of course, there are many who exercise their gifts in quiet ways for God. Keeping a rosebed tidy in the churchyard is a lovely thing to do; so is making a cup of tea or coffee at a parish function; so is reading the Epistle at the Eucharist; so is arranging the flowers; so, most certainly, is the delivery of magazines and the consequent visiting of some who may have no other real contact with the Church. These things may give pleasure to many, and how very much we value those who give their talents in this kind of way.

But, important though these things are, it may be that there are other gifts which God wishes us to use in service to his Church. Many congregations contain people whose highly responsible jobs affect the lives of thousands; people who are experts in communication—teachers, journalists, even broadcasters; people who are expert counsellors, not qualified, just ordinary people who are ready quietly to listen and help. This list could go on and on. What a world of talent we have in the Church! But do we use it?

An appeal

It may well be that the time has come to surprise each other, to ask ourselves very earnestly, 'Have I a special gift to use more in God's service?' Who knows where that question, properly asked, could end? It is quite certain that if our parochial church councils were looking properly at *this* aspect of ministry, then the Church of God would be changed dramatically in its mission to this nation and beyond.

EIGHTH SUNDAY BEFORE EASTER

The church on a journey

Mark 7.24 *Then he left that place and went away into the territory of Tyre*

We may often think of Jesus as meeting hundreds of different people in various places as he journeyed around Palestine; indeed his ministry gives a vivid impression of being on the move. This particular text gives me a chance to talk about journeying.

1 *To stand firm or cut loose*

Over and over again I am asked, as many Christian leaders are asked, to 'give a lead' on some matter of public concern, and sometimes one is able to say something of some small value, if one agrees with what has been said. Those, who urge the clergy to assume the prophet's mantle, often have clear, but alas!, conflicting ideas of what he ought to be saying, if my experience is anything to go by. Some tell me that the message ought to be 'stand firm', to insist on the old and tried ways of expressing the Christian faith, for a bewildered world needs at least the Church to stand firm.

Others will say that this is the time to cut loose from the past old ways of thinking; to be bold enough to immerse ourselves in the present, where we shall find God's will for us in contemporary struggles, injustice and bigotry.

59

I am unwilling to surrender to either of these positions, although I recognize that they are both built around important truths, but 'stand firm' is not the whole answer, because the old words do not touch the experience of many of our contemporaries. The children of 'stand firm' parents show an alarming tendency to cut loose! But total immersion in the present and its struggles cannot be the way for us as a Church, either. If it were, we should cease to be the salt seasoning the whole and a transforming influence upon the world around. We should become merely a dull echo of the latest fashionable indignation. In my experience the children of the trendy often show a surprising thirst for tradition.

We are on the journey at a time when our contemporaries are unconvinced by neat and tidy descriptions of religious truth; search and quest and experiment are the order of the day. We have stackable chairs, not fixed pews; we offer worship with disposable booklets, not bound books. At such a time, to stand firm with old thoughts and words could make the Church a ghetto for the timid, but to capitulate to fashionable cynicism, to limp aimlessly after the fads and fashions of the world, would be to betray the vision that makes our life a journey.

2 *A journey through time*

There is a third option for us—one which does not neglect the past or the present, but which brings them into fruitful interplay with each other and the future. I believe that the Church must recover a vivid sense of being on a journey through time. We are the people to whom God has assigned a journey. We dare not say that we have arrived with all the answers, nor dare we abandon our own course to follow passing fashions.

The Bible is full of the spirit of journeying. God's people have always been on the move: the exodus from Egypt, the exile from the promised land, Paul's travels through the Roman world. These were journeys in both a geographical and also a spiritual sense. The deepend vision, which came to God's people in the desert, beside the waters of Babylon, and in taking their experiences of Jesus to the nations, had a transforming effect upon them; and, through them, on the history of the world.

The mediaeval Church believed that it possessed a framework which could embrace and interpret every human experience. There was often little sense that the Church should be alert to discern the spirit leading her to new understanding of the truth. In consequence, the Church atrophied, became hollow and brittle, and finally collapsed and split tragically apart. We have great ruined or partially destroyed churches all over the country to point to that collapse. We dare not believe that we understand everything and that 'stand firm' is the only sufficient message for our time.

As a child I was brought up in a parish that was greatly influenced by Father Hebert and his emphasis upon the Parish Communion movement. Tentatively, in the twenties, the incumbent of that parish (as also the incumbents of many other parishes), introduced a simple Parish Communion service to replace Matins, which was at that time well-nigh universal within the Church of England. What that journey has meant for the Church of England, in terms of a greater understanding of the importance of Christ's command, to 'Do this', is incalculable in its benefits.

3 A journey in hope and confidence

We do not know where that road will take us, but we must set out with the hope and confidence that can be learnt from the journey so far. We must not, in panic, abandon all that we have gathered along the way, but we must not be so attached to the customs and traditional ways of understanding, which we have inherited, that we are prevented from venturing further. Some of the baggage must be left behind if we are to make progress. People will argue about what is baggage and what are essential supplies, but if the Church can again adopt its journeying frame of mind—hopeful, resolutely committed to the vision, free from the tyranny of present conditions and difficulties—then I believe it will have the energy and the spirit to move mountains, and the gates of hell will not prevail against such a Church.

SEVENTH SUNDAY BEFORE EASTER

Christ, the Friend of Sinners

John 8.5 *'Moses laid down that such women are to be stoned. What do you say about it?'*

Whenever this beautiful and terrible story is read publicly in church there is a duty to preach about it, because it was evidently felt in the early Church that it should never be read without comment.

The narrative of the guilty wife seems to have been part of the apostolic preaching, which the teachers of the first age hesitated to incorporate into a written gospel. It appeared in some copies of St Luke's Gospel, but it finally found a place in St John's. It was often left out in some copies, apparently on the score that, although our Lord forbade a repetition of the woman's sin, his tenderness towards her might lead to laxity when it was explained.

1 *The story*

Think of this incident. Our Lord was never more brutally treated than on this occasion. The incident showed a most horrible spirit, because the question asked was not a practical one. Those people were not on the way to deliver the guilty wife up to justice. There was no such punishment for adultery in the time of our Lord. It was all mere cruelty and wicked sport. This evidently happened when Jerusalem was crowded for one of the great feasts, probably the Feast of Tabernacles. There was always a certain amount of sin and licence at the great feasts, owing to the herding of multitudes of people together. It was not only the religious who fulfilled their religious duties among the Jews. The duties were a political obligation, and the crowd round Jerusalem at these times had some of the elements in it of a crowd surrounding Nelson's Column in Trafalgar Square on a national occasion. This unfortunate woman had sinned and been found out. An exulting group of external moralists is a disgusting body of people, and that is what they were. Nobody, who really felt the sinfulness of sin, could have acted in this way.

Then some brilliant person, who had a hatred of our Lord, conceived the idea of cornering him on a question of morals, while he was teaching in the temple. He knew our Lord would not sympathize with them and he thought that, if our Lord failed to show sympathy with this apparent zeal for morals, he would suffer in the eyes of those who surrounded him. So the group was delighted to have got such a chance, dragging the unhappy woman up into the temple, forced their way through our Lord's attentive congregation, stopped his sermon and stood the woman in the middle of the big semi-circle and put their question, 'What do you say?'

Our Lord looked neither at the accusers nor at the woman. He did not strike an attitude of discussion nor did he preserve an offended silence. It was as though he was altogether unconscious of their presence and question. After a little while he stooped down and, apparently, traced some letters on the pavement. We do not know what he wrote, but such a strange act would create, as it continued, a stillness and a tension. It evidently went on for some time, because the narrative says that the accusers repeated their question time after time. At last our Lord raised himself and then he looked at them all and said to them: 'That one of you who is faultless shall throw the first stone.' Then once again he bent down and wrote on the ground. The second writing frightened the accusers. They may have thought our Lord was writing curses against them, weaving some spell, 'setting the runes' upon them, as our pagan forefathers would have said. So they began to slip off through the crowd one by one, no doubt making various excuses to one another for doing so, and we may imagine what those might have been. 'You see,' one might have said, 'how impossible it is to get a straight answer out of him'; or another, 'Look at him; he is evidently mad'; or a third, 'We wasted our time; he cannot take up any challenge'. However this may have been, they slip away, leaving the gaping folk who had been there before; and among them only the two chief figures in the recent scene—our Lord and the woman.

But our Lord wrote on apparently for some time, and still there was a silence and a tension. Presently our Lord lifted himself up again and looked now for the first time at the woman, and said to her with gravity: 'Where are they? Has no one condemned you?' And she said, 'No one, sir.' Jesus said, 'Nor do I condemn you. You may go; do not sin again.'

2 *The lesson of history*

St Augustine says that our Lord here condemns the sin but not the human being. To the human being, who had undergone the frightful punishment of exposure, he gives another chance. So far he treats her as he treats you and me; but if you would study our Lord's teaching about the class of sin which this woman had committed, then you must look in another part of the Gospels. 'If your eye offends you . . .', says our Lord. If there is one aspect of your general point of view, which looks in the direction of sensuality, then get rid of it. It may curtail your interests, but it is better to go through life with only half your sight than to range freely over all the landscape here and to lose life altogether.

Our Lord does not condemn us for any sin any more than he condemned this woman in the temple. To all he gives another chance, but we must seek his presence. We must ask for his forgiveness.

LENT 1

Applying ourselves in Lent

Luke 4.4 *Jesus answered, 'Scripture says, "Man cannot live on bread alone."'*

St Benedict tells us that in Lent we have 'apply' ourselves, which, in simple terms, means not so much to do extraordinary things as to concentrate on getting ordinary things right. That is sound commonsense advice as we keep another Lent; and there are a few simple ways in which we ought to be applying ourselves.

1 *We must learn to accept the givenness of things around us*

Our job; our responsibilities; our family obligations; the shortcomings of those who annoy us; the irritation of tasks which are uncongenial; and all the many and varied aspects of life which are part of the day-to-day situation in which God has set us. We must never forget that we are called to serve God in 'the present moment'—not regretting the past; not always wishing that we were doing something different.

2 *We must learn to be more thankful*

How different we look and feel if we learn to recognize and rejoice in all that is good and true and beautiful. This, too, is based on the givenness of life. At the end of every day look back and identify all the good things and the people who have brought a little light and joy into life. Be awake and aware of the support of friends; the love of family; the kindness of a stranger; the helpfulness of someone in a shop; health of body and mind; the courage of someone who is ill; the healing of a broken relationship. The list is endless. Try making your own list over a day or a week and offer it all to God in thanksgiving as part of his creative love.

3 *We must learn to accept our own inadequacies*

Lent has been described as 'six weeks of honesty with ourselves'. How often do we put on a mask for ourselves as well as for others? Accepting ourselves as we really are does not lead to despondency but rather to great peace. It is only when we are honest about ourselves that we can recognize and accept the loving mercy and goodness of God, and so enable him to do his work within us and through us. God wants not our ability so much as our availability.

4 *We must be ready to relax*

This is not only a matter for those whose lives are very full. Sometimes people, who have plenty of time, are tense and anxious. So we have to learn to 'let go'. It is God's world and we cannot solve the problems of the world by anxious fretting. For those who live full and busy lives we have to make time 'to waste with God'. Do not imagine that you can bring in the kingdom on your own—or to-morrow. Learn patience; be tolerant with others; be relaxed and open in your relationships; be ready and prepared for the opportunities and tasks of each day, to tackle them with quiet and relaxed poise.

5 *We must learn to look at the needs of others*

But again we must be relaxed about this and not constantly taking our own caring temperature. We are to be channels of God's love, not of our own feeble love. God's love has been poured into our hearts by the Holy Spirit. Accept this love and let it flow freely to meet the needs of others.

When we are lonely or ill or anxious, it is easy to give way to self-pity, but then try to look away from yourself, for the best cure is attending to the needs of others and becoming an instrument of God's love and peace. In the Book of Deuteronomy (9.3) God is described thus: 'The Lord your God is he who goes before you.' When things are difficult, hold fast to those words and you will have something to share with the next person you meet.

So, through this Lent keep on looking ahead hopefully. Concentrate on the risen Christ and think about him joyfully. We must go to the foot of the cross, but that is not the end of the road. Lent leads us through Good Friday to Easter Day.

LENT 2

Conflict and peace

> Matthew 12.26 *'And if it is Satan who casts out Satan, Satan is divided against himself; how then can his kingdom stand?'*

1 *Conflict*

Today's readings are all about conflict and an unquiet world. In every parish church we offer up regularly that simple prayer to Almighty God, 'Give peace in our time, O Lord.' Nothing is prayed for more than peace nowadays, but often we may feel that nothing seems more unlikely than that we should enjoy lasting peace in this haunted, unquiet civilization of ours. The twentieth century has been, perhaps, the most violent century that the world has ever known. Christians believe that peace in a non-Christian world is, in fact, an illusion; unredeemed men and women cannot help living in a state of mutual hostility because of the very nature of the case. Most people, it is certain, ardently desire peace, but they have little or no wish to take seriously to the Christian religion, which is the one vital essential of a peaceful world.

The events of history teach us much. Recently I was reading of an address given by Mr Balfour, when he was Prime Minister, to the University of Edinburgh, early in this century. He was invited to speak on the subject of 'The Moral values which unite nations'. In his address he spoke of the different ties which bind together the peoples of the world, ties of common knowledge, of commerce, of diplomatic relationships and the ordinary bonds of human friendship. When he had finished speaking, a young Japanese student, studying at the University, asked a question. 'But, Mr Balfour, what about Jesus Christ in all this?' There was dead silence as all those present felt the justice of the rebuke. The leading statesman of a reputedly Christian nation had been dealing with the ties that can unite all men in world brotherhood and peace, and he had left out the one essential bond.

How many really want peace in this way? Probably only a very few modern men and women realize just how much the modern, peaceful civilization, which they so ardently desire, depends upon the Christian faith for its existence.

2 *The way to peace*

The worst kind of religion is no religion at all; and modern men and women, enjoying the benefits of civilized life and indulging in the amusement of going without a religion, ought to be thankful that they live in a land, where the Gospel of Jesus has largely tamed the beastliness and the ferocity of their fellow men. But for Christianity they might long ago have eaten their carcases as the South Sea Islanders did; or cut off their heads as did the monsters of the French Revolution; or sent to gas chambers those of other nations and beliefs as did those of the Nazi revolution; or despatched those who refused to conform to the State's way, by sending them for prolonged and ghastly treatment of rehabilitation as the Russian Communists are still doing today.

We Christians challenge any modern atheist to show us any place on earth, ten miles square, where a man may live in decency and security, supporting and educating his children, a place where age is reverenced and human life is held in due regard, where the Gospel of Christ has not gone first and cleared the way, laid the foundations and made decency and security possible.

If you really want civilization and peace, then there is only one way open to obtain those things: The salvation of Jesus Christ on the large scale, putting men into a right relationship with Almighty God and, as a natural follow-up to that, putting them into a right relationship with one another.

It is commonly said that you cannot legislate above the average morality of the people for whom you are responsible; that is to say, public opinion is the real law of nations. Very well then; the truth is that the Christian opinion and determination of ordinary men and women can have a far more profound effect upon world affairs than all the forlorn intentions and sorry speeches of international politics.

LENT 3

Solitude

> Matthew 16.24 *Jesus said, 'If anyone wishes to be a follower of mine, he must leave self behind; he must take up his cross and come with me.'*

1 *Lonely, but not alone*

Occasionally I am driven to re-read some outstanding sermons of really great men. Such a one is Paul Tillich's celebrated sermon, 'Loneliness and Solitude'. I was driven to re-read it by an experience of a young student recently confirmed. At that great event for him, no member of his family was there to support him, for his parents and other relatives had not sufficient interest in his Confirmation to bring them to Church on that evening. When I sought to see them I was rebuffed. This young man's interest in the Christian faith has since aroused considerable hostility from his father. Incidents of this sort are more numerous than I happen to know about. Recently a suffragan bishop said that, when he confirmed a group of young married women, not one was supported by her husband. They were mostly indifferent and some were hostile. I am, therefore, today speaking of four consequent thoughts.

First, how lonely it can be to be a Christian nowadays. On occasion it has always been a lonely business, let us say, to be known and recognized, at school or in the Forces or at work, as a praying and worshipping Christian; and now, increasingly, it may be a lonely business at home as well.

This leads us on, secondly, to the essential loneliness of human beings. This is something deep in our human condition, not the only factor but, nevertheless, a factor to be recognized, and much in our modern life accentuates this. Increased social mobility, the decreasing importance of the extended family, the ever-present spectre of unemployment, all serve to make this loneliness especially poignant for more and more people today.

2 *Fellowship of warmth*

These two reflections provide the background for another reflection. Certain features of modern church life are explicable in terms of these two considerations. For instance, increasingly we find handshakes, and even embraces, in church, especially at the offertory in the Holy Communion service. We have opportunities for worshippers to meet socially for coffee or breakfast after Sunday worship, sometimes within the church building itself. The palpable warmth of human fellowship is thus pervading many groups of Christian people. If by temperament, upbringing or habit you do not take kindly to some of these developments, then I ask you to understand them and to sympathize with them as a means of providing the assurance, the spirit and the friendship, which even a generation ago most Christian people in this country would have found either in their family or within the general framework of society. Many people are now looking to the Church to provide that which they cannot readily find elsewhere, for loneliness is a great scourge today.

And now these words about Jesus in St Matthew's Gospel were, we are told, that 'he sent the multitudes away and went into a mountain to pray; and when the evening was come he was there alone.' In Jesus' life both company and solitude played their part. In any human life the corporate and the individual complement one another. In church life the communal features, to which I have just drawn attention, do not stand by themselves, nor as ends in themselves. Viewed properly, they are what we might call sacraments of encouragement and assurance, which God provides for us in the life of faith. They can warm us; they can assist us; they can lead us on to deeper faith and hope. Therefore, in the concluding words of Paul Tillich's sermon, 'Let us dare to have solitude—to face the eternal, to find others and to see ourselves.'

LENT 4

Loneliness and companionship

> Matthew 17.2 *Jesus led them up a high mountain . . . and in their presence he was transfigured.*

Today's Gospel commemorates one of the most noble events in our Lord's earthly life—the transfiguration. In each of the first three Gospels this story is told and is closely associated with the incident at Caesarea Philippi when Peter recognized the Messiahship of his Master and made a confession. This was followed by the words of Jesus foretelling the journey to the cross. For each of the writers of the synoptic Gospels the transfiguration took place at the turning-point in Christ's ministry. It was the first clear, decisive step on the road to Calvary.

What was it then that happened when Jesus took with him Peter and John and James and went up into the mountain to pray? Most of us, if we were asked to describe the transfiguration, would probably say that it was the occasion when his clothes became white and dazzling.

1 *Two visitors*

But this is not its real significance. It is indeed quite likely that a similar transfiguration took place on other occasions, and some might believe that it happened every time he turned aside to pray. But on this occasion, instead of being alone in prayer, as was his custom, he had the three disciples with him. Quite naturally, his shining face and glowing garments attracted the disciples' riveted attention, as it has done the attention of the readers of the records ever since. But the thing that mattered then and matters now was not the change in appearance and apparel, but another feature of the event altogether. 'They saw Moses and Elijah appear, conversing with him and speaking of his death which he was to fulfil at Jerusalem.' This was the important feature of the transfiguration: the appearance of these two visitors from the spirit world and the theme of their conversation, the approaching sacrifice of Calvary.

2 *Loneliness*

These two may be described as the great typical figures of the Old Testament. Moses and Elijah belonged to different ages of the far past and apparently had nothing in common with each other. Moses was learned in all the culture of Egyptian civilization: Elijah was a rough man of the wilderness. What was common between them, however, was that both of them had known what it was to be alone in the midst of ingratitude and misunderstanding, with none to whom they could turn for sympathy; and both had found their strength in God.

In this these two very different men were not only linked to one another but to the Saviour himself. Great men are always lonely; it is one of the penalties of being called to supreme position. If that is true of those who occupy prominent positions in the affairs of the world, it is vastly more true of him who discovered his unique lot among the sons of men.

3 Comradeship

He knew that the agelong purpose of God centred in him, that he was the long-expected Messiah and Redeemer of the world. There was no man on earth, with whom he could share that secret notion, who would have understood him, if he had spoken of it. In his great sermon on 'The Loneliness of Christ', Robertson of Brighton said, 'Those who understood him best only half understood him; those who knew him best scarcely could be said to know him at all.' And so, when our Lord went into the mountain to pray, it appears that God answered his prayer by sending to his aid these two faithful servants of his, both of whom had graduated in the school of loneliness and whose solitude had been created by their unswerving loyalty to God. In their company Jesus found the comradeship of those who could understand his mission, his circumstances and his need, and fortify him for what lay ahead. He knew and they knew that the eternal purpose of God, worked out through law and prophets, was to be continued and consummated by suffering and sacrifice.

So law and prophecy met on the mountain and bore their witness to him as the Messiah. The road to the Cross lay plain before him, and so from that time 'he steadfastly set his face to go to Jerusalem'. The vision passed, the conversation ended; but the comfort and strength it brought to the lonely heart of Jesus remained with him to the end.

LENT 5

A costly stand

> Mark 10.39 *Jesus said, 'The baptism I am baptized with shall be your baptism.'*

Not long ago I baptized, prior to their Confirmation, three young men and two young women from a current marriage preparation forum. As is frequent nowadays, they had not been baptized as babies, because their parents had decided 'to let them choose for themselves later on'. Whatever the virtues of that decision, in the economy of God it led to some remarkable commitments from those five young adults and a full realization of the toughness of the witness they were now called to in crossing the divide from paganism to Christian commitment.

In common with many parish priests, I find that classes for adult Baptism and adult Confirmation are larger than ever before, often calling for considerable courage in the candidates. Some, like James and John in today's Gospel, have to face the fact that Christ is calling for a reassessment of their values, and they discover that to be a committed Christian is a job involving utter dedication.

1 *Courage to stand out*

For it takes courage to live the Christian life, and nobody who is weak in character can be called a good Christian. The idea that Christianity is a religion for the senile is now fast dying, and it is indeed strange that it ever arose. Perhaps there was a confusion in some people's minds between the words, 'weak' and 'meek'. Our Lord said, 'Blessed are the meek.' He certainly did not say, 'Blessed are the weak.' Meek is the same word as humble, and only the greatest characters are humble.

Our Lord himself was never weak. He stood out against all the most powerful forces of his time and against all the most influential people. Where this has been called for, his followers have done this all down the ages, from St Paul and St Peter to outstanding pastors like Niemöller during the Nazi regime in Germany, and great bishops like Archbishop Luwum who was martyred for withstanding a vicious Ugandan regime; and hundreds of Christ's followers in this century have been prepared to take the consequences. To those who are inspired rather than daunted by the difficulties of serving Christ there is given the opportunity of taking the definite step of Confirmation. Without question, many are taking this step today with a sense of much greater commitment than has been the case in the past, and some remarkable young people are entering the Church of God through this means.

2 *Confirming the stance*

Confirmation candidates come both to confirm and to be confirmed. They *confirm* the promises made for them in their baptism (or made by them in their baptism if they are baptized as adults), and they come *to be confirmed* through strength from the presence of God in their hearts. In Confirmation we first pledge ourselves to lead a Christian life in the presence of the congregation and in the sight of God. The promises themselves are easy enough to say and to remember. Briefly, they are to give up what is wrong; to believe what is true; and to do what is right. But God knows that the promises, although easy to say, are very hard to keep; and so, in Confirmation, God offers his help by coming to dwell in our hearts.

This is not magic. No sudden recognizable change takes place in those who are newly-confirmed. To anyone meeting them they appear very much the same as before; but a seed has been sown. You can dig up two flower beds and prepare them. You can then sow seed in one of them. For a while there is no difference, but in the end flowers grow in one and nothing in the other. It is true that nothing will grow in either of the beds if you omit to water them and care for them; but however much care you may take nothing will grow, except weeds, in the one that has no planted seed.

God, the Holy Spirit, makes this great offer to come and dwell with us and help us, if we will open the door. Some of you may know the picture, 'The Light of the World'. If you look at it closely, you see that there is no handle on the door, on which our Lord is knocking. The only handle on that door is on the inside. The painter was wise. Christ will not open the door of your heart by force. You must open it to him.

3 *Take time to decide*

One of the off-putting facts which can sometimes daunt those considering Confirmation is that friends have been confirmed and have fallen back. God knows there are too many of them in church today, but this should not be a worry. Preparation for Confirmation these days is over a long period—five or six months at least, when the priest explains as fully as he can what the Christian life means. There may be two reasons why you may not be confirmed; one, that you yourself do not feel called to the disciplines of Confirmation, or secondly, that the preparing priest may advise you not to go forward at this stage. But there is plenty of time to make a decision. There is no conscription in this war, but to those who have not faced this particular call there is a clear opportunity to take up arms for Christ and his Church, by pledging ourselves thus in his service and so receiving his great help in Confirmation.

PALM SUNDAY

A decisive week

> Matthew 21.10–11 *When he entered Jerusalem the whole city went wild with excitement. 'Who is this?' people asked, and the crowd replied, 'This is the prophet Jesus, from Nazareth in Galilee.'*

Today is Palm Sunday. It is the beginning of a decisive week, Holy Week, and this is the one week out of the whole of human history, of which Christians possess a detailed diary. What could be more right then than to commemorate the last week of Christ's earthly life?

1 *A planned week*

Look into the stories of the week. You notice one big feature. As far as Jesus is concerned this was a planned week; deliberately he faced it and went through with it. To begin with, on this Palm Sunday he rode into Jerusalem, with all those men, women and children cheering; but that was no accident. He sent out a party the day before, who were to find an ass tied and a colt with her. 'Just give the password,' he ordered, 'then loose them and bring them to me.'

The people hailed him as an earthly king, who should lead them against the Romans; but our Lord in the four days that followed quickly dispelled their illusions. 'Straightway', we are told by St Luke, 'he entered into the temple to cast out them that sold, saying, "It is written: My house shall be a house of prayer, but you have made it a den of robbers".'

St Luke's account goes on significantly, 'He was teaching daily in the temple, but the chief priests and the scribes and the principal men of the people sought to destroy him, and they could not find a way to do it, for the people all hung upon his words.' Chapters 20 and 21 of St Luke's Gospel are filled with our Lord's teaching in the temple during those fateful four days, and at the end of the account of the Lord's talks, the words are: 'And every day he was teaching in the temple, but every night he went out and came to the Mount of Olives.'

Later in the week, on the Thursday in the evening, he offered to his friends those amazing mysteries of body and blood and bread and wine—that supreme sacrament, which is an ever-available sign of our redemption from sin. 'And then he went out, as his custom was, to the Mount of Olives and the disciples followed him.' He chose his three best men to help him through, just as we ask for the prayers of our dearest friends when we are up against a crisis. So we see our Lord enduring great agonies of indecision within him: 'Father, remove this cup from me if it is possible. Nevertheless, not my will but thine be done.'

2 *A purposeful week*

Meanwhile those three best men fell asleep. It certainly was not that they did not want to follow their master. The spirit was willing but they were tired out; they lacked the energy. There are many these days who are worn out, or simply lacking the energy and vigilance that is needed to be a follower of Christ. To be a follower of our Lord is a task requiring very great energy and one which always requires his help, for there is a constant fight between our guardian angel and our personal devil. We need our Holy Week to awake from out of lethargy.

Later this week Christians will hear the magnificent Passion narratives read in the Gospels, and then assemble to commemorate the first Good Friday and especially the words Jesus said, 'It is finished.' Epstein took hold of that phrase and, using his skill as a sculptor, he froze the phrase into a great block of alabaster, which was to be a symbolic figure of Christ, lying flat, stone cold and dead, and around the sides of it the chisel chipped the words, 'consummatum est' (it is finished); but that is not what Jesus meant.

I happen to be an admirer of Waterloo Bridge, which I

watched growing almost daily as an undergraduate. Put yourself in the position of the men who built that bridge. Can you picture them standing to look when they had completed their job? 'It is finished,' undoubtedly they said. Finished, yes, but not finished *with*; completed they would mean, ready and finished for use. Across the bridge, the traffic could pass.

The Christian faith is God's bridging scheme in history, and on the cross God completed the task. This was *how* God completed it, for only if God had crossed to us can we hope to cross to him. Deliberately, therefore, Jesus became man; deliberately he came over to our side of the gap to share the pain and the evil and the mud, and now he offers us the bridge of his own life, so that we may in our turn cross to God. 'My life,' he was saying there, 'is finished'; finished for mankind to share and to use. 'For I am come that they might have life and have it more abundantly.'

3 *A week calling for our response*

Our response to that is the response of *faith*. It is simple and straightforward. It includes owning up to one's sins, which make the gap. It includes a firm intention to *live*; in other words, to *use* the life which is the bridge across the gap. It includes regular and reverent reading of God's word in the Bible. It includes faithful attendance at the service Jesus gave to us—in the Holy Communion. At heart it is simple and straightforward enough. It is exactly the faith which you put in any bridge builder when you walk across his bridge.

Finally, let me urge you again to do something every day in this week. In your Prayer Book you will find a different Gospel for every day in this week, describing the events leading to the death and resurrection of our Lord and Master. Do, please, read them some time during each day for which they are written. It will take you fifteen minutes each day, but it will prepare you wonderfully for your Easter Communion. If you can possibly do so, be in church to hear those Gospels read in the context of the

Eucharist. If you do this you will find that next Sunday, when we joyously proclaim God's victory over sin and evil, you are infinitely better prepared, because in some small measure you will have shared in the Passion of our Lord and Master.

EASTER DAY

No waste

John 6.12 *'Collect the pieces left over, so that nothing may be lost.'*

Easter is literally too big for words. The machinery of language breaks down under the weight of glory. We read of the women who fled from the empty tomb, that they said nothing to anyone. Words and thought itself could not stand the strain of Christ's resurrection.

Yet man is a thinking animal and, therefore, an inquisitive one. He was bound to ask: 'What does Christ's resurrection mean?' And the Church had to provide an answer. But since the resurrection passes beyond the range of man's capacity to think, the Church, in order to explain it, had to split it up. It was like splitting up a chord into component notes and considering one note at a time; and that is all we can do in one sermon such as this—consider one note in the great chord of Easter.

1 *Fragmentation*

Let us take note today of death. Death means disintegration. A corpse is a body falling to pieces. The hand of death pulls apart what should be bound together. In these days, the hand of death is so obviously laid upon our world. On all sides, we have evidence of death's disintegrating pressure. The machine of the world's economics, we know, is dangerously out of gear. The threat of war always seems to be dancing like an uncontrollable dervish in and out of the ranks of the world's politicians. In some places the fabric of Christian civilization has crumbled. All this has its effects upon our individual lives. Men and women, who are older, are not so easily giving themselves steadily and without interruption to their life's work, nor do they hope to see at its end a panorama of beneficent results. Can a young doctor, for example, hope when he is old to see the world a happier place because of the exercise of his healing art? He may well ask himself: 'Is it worth trying to heal and to build as one sees how strong are the forces bent upon warring and pulling down?' The same question in a different form can be heard in many young homes today. Is it worth bringing up a family when the fruit of one's effort and sacrifice may be plucked away before it is even ripe? We cannot escape the fact that the hand of death laid upon our world is waiting to pull in pieces the work of our lives.

Why then do we sing 'Alleluia' today? Are we just poor, idle singers on an empty day—drinking spiritual brandy in order to forget the futility of all that we do? Of course, the answer is 'No!' But have we discovered why it is 'No'? We sing, not to forget, but because we remember. We remember that on the first Easter Day there went forth from the Father's throne the royal command, 'Collect the pieces left over, so that nothing may be lost.'

2 Disintegration

Think of the body of Jesus, lying a corpse in the tomb. That corpse was a symbol of his whole earthly career. He was really dead, so disintegration must have begun to set in. This disintegration symbolized a life's work dissolved into fragments. The real career of Jesus had certainly been no royal progress. It did not elicit a steady, increasing response. It did not grow firmly in strength and influence. The crowds listened, wondered; and went away. The five thousand were fed and subsequently disbelieved. The evangelistic campaign of the twelve and the seventy seems

81

to have done little else than create temporary excitement. The seed of miracle and parable, so liberally scattered, produced nothing that could be called a harvest, but only a few individual and rather poor stalks of corn. The triumphal entry on Palm Sunday petered out miserably. The band of the apostles fell to pieces; the most intelligent betrayed our Lord; the most affectionate denied him. Jesus had come into the world to bring mankind back to God. What, in fact, had he done? He had healed various people here and there, people who had gone back to their homes and disappeared. He had blessed a few children. He had collected a rather tattered band of followers, insignificant both in number and in station. He had rescued a prostitute. He had made a rich young man think. He had angered a college of priests. He had given a Roman civil servant a half-hour's interesting conversation. He had comforted a dying scoundrel. Sent into the world to save the millions of mankind, his work in the end amounted to a few scattered fragments. Each thing in itself, of course, worthwhile, but all hopelessly unco-ordinated. Finally, the instrument of his work, his body, became a sacrifice, a victim of dissolution. The hand of death, stretched out over his entire ministry, at last came down and killed him when he was thirty-three years old.

3 *Resurrection*

But in God's kingdom there can be no waste. Nothing, however small, however isolated, can ever drop from the Father's hand. What time and death put asunder, God joins together; so Christ was raised from the dead, and the dissolving particles of a corpse were gathered up and remade into a body of glory, and the bits and the pieces of a disjointed ministry were wonderfully woven together into a garment of salvation for the whole world. In the person of the risen Saviour the Trinity took up the scattered fragments of time and made them part of its own indestructible unity. The Resurrection means that the events of the Gospel story, dispersed in time and place, will now for ever as a single pattern attain the mansions of heaven.

Application

And we here today are members of the risen Christ. In baptism we were given to him by the Father, and the Father's will is that 'Of all which he has given me, I should lose nothing but should raise it up at the last day.' This means that nothing good which we have attempted, no service to our fellow men, no effort to heal and to build, no sacrifice of comfort and convenience, no conquest within ourselves of pride and jealousy—it is the Father's will that none of these things shall be lost. 'I will raise it up'—so runs the promise of Christ.

Thus, Christian people have never given up the attempt to make the world a better place, however strong the evil that has opposed them, however restricted their sphere of activity, however broken and scattered their work, because Christ died, and behold he lives! He is the resurrection and, therefore, he is able to gather all scattered efforts and to take them into the unity of his risen person.

Hence the unquenchable vitality of the Church which is his body—always in the darkest moments planning the conquest of new worlds. The Church goes on, though adversaries have demolished it a thousand times in arguments and pronounced it a dead thing and cried to carry out the corpse, for all was over but the shouting; and they have begun the shouting, only to find when it was over that the slain Hydra had raised a new head and all was to begin again, because the Lord is risen and the Easter hope is inexhaustible.

EASTER 1

The Feast of Friendship

John 6.35 *Jesus said to them, 'I am the bread of life.'*

There comes to most of us in life the moment when, for the first time, we realize our need of God. Sometimes it comes to us simply through a feeling of the vastness of the universe. In face of its terrifying and often ruthless forces we feel our own human frailty and long for the support of something or someone greater or more wise, more tender, more pitiful. Sometimes it comes to us as the result of some crushing sorrow, such as the loss of a dear friend, when we realize that we live in a world of change and insecurity and long for something that does not change and to which we can hold with absolute confidence; or perhaps still more often we discover our own need of God through our sins and failures. Despite all our good resolutions we blunder and fall and hurt ourselves and hurt others. Then we realize that we need a greater strength than our own strength, if we are to be able to stand up to the testing ordeals of life and the dangerous powers of evil. So we long for God.

1 *The Sacrament of God's friendship*

As soon as we feel our need for God he meets us halfway. Far more than we ever long for his help, he longs for our love, and is waiting to come to our rescue and reveal himself to us. Now God has provided different ways in which we can receive his help or, to use a theological word, his grace. One way is through prayer, another through the Bible, another through the worship and the fellowship of the Church, but the most important way is through that rite, which has been observed by Christians all down the ages and which we call the Holy Communion or the Sacrament of the Lord's Supper. In it we are more surely in touch with God than at any other time on earth.

You cannot really understand what Holy Communion

is unless you go right back in imagination to the beginnings of Christianity and see where and how it started. The first Lord's Supper took place under unforgettable circumstances. It was the last day in the earthly life of our Lord. He had, as usual been very busy all day teaching, preaching, healing, giving interviews to people about all sorts and conditions of things; but after all this he had carefully kept time free for a last intimate talk with his twelve special friends. As arranged by the Master, they met in a quiet upper room at Jerusalem. The doors were shut; the lamps were lit. After supper a hush fell upon the little company, for there was a sense of impending danger. They all knew that their beloved leader and friend, because of his fearless loyalty to truth, had many enemies in high places, and that those enemies were at that very moment plotting to kill him. Across the group of friends, even in the peace and light of that upper room, lay the shadow of the cross.

Then out of the silence the Master spoke. Taking into his hands a loaf of bread, he broke it and said, 'Take, eat; this is my body which is broken for you; do this in remembrance of me.' Lifting a cup of wine from the table he said, 'This is the new covenant in my blood, shed for the remission of the sins of many. Drink it all of you, you are my friends. Greater love has no man than this; that a man lays down his life for his friends.'

2 Friendship at its highest

They only dimly understood what he meant, but they did understand that here was friendship at its deepest and at its highest. The next day they understood a little more of what he meant when they saw their dear Master hanging on a cross on that hilltop outside the city walls; his body indeed broken and torn by the nails, his blood gushing out as the spear of a Roman soldier pierced his side. This man, the only sinless man who ever walked our earth, a victim to the selfishness and cruelty of sinful man, allowing himself voluntarily to be killed, as it were, for the sins of the whole world.

That strange rite, that solemn feast of friendship in the upper room at Jerusalem, has been kept by the friends of Christ all down the centuries. It has become the supreme act of worship and fellowship in the life of the Christian Church. We cannot even now understand half of what it means, but we do know that at that table Christ, our Saviour, meets with us as his friends, 'unseen but not unknown', and that through broken bread and poured out wine he gives to us something of his strength and love to equip us for the battle of daily existence. Thus his own divine life somehow actually lives in us.

3 *The demands of this friendship*

But there is something more which we dare not forget. Jesus said, 'You are my friends if you do what I command you.' Friendship is an exciting thing. It has its responsibilities as well as privileges and joys. Christ, our divine friend, always sends us out from the quiet of the upper room, out from the peace of the Church, into the stormy, dangerous arena of the common world—there to live out the Christian life, the life of unselfish service, of unflinching loyalty to the truth, because the servant is not greater than his Lord. Unless it gives us courage and endurance, unselfishness and purity of heart in the relationships of ordinary life, then the Sacrament is no more than a sham. But if, as often as we have the chance, we come in humble faith to receive his sacramental gift, then it does give us power to overcome our temptations and to show in our daily conduct something at least of the gentleness and strength and valour and love, that shone out so wonderfully in the earthly life of Christ, our Saviour.

EASTER 2

Pastoral work

John 10.11 *'I am the good shepherd'*

In St John's Gospel we have a series of sayings of Jesus beginning 'I am'. We all know them: 'I am the good shepherd'; 'I am the light of the world'; 'I am the resurrection' and 'I am life', and so on. It is almost as though Jesus is answering the question, 'Who do you think you are?' These statements about himself are only recorded in the fourth Gospel and leave us tremendously in that evangelist's debt.

1 *The Shepherd image*

Today we look at the claim, 'I am the good shepherd.' The image of a shepherd was certainly highly relevant to the people to whom he spoke. In our great conurbations today one might expect quite a different image to be used, but the image was far more than just topical. It was brimful of association for the devout Jew of the time. Ever since the days of David the image of shepherd and sheep had been used to describe the relationship of God and the people of Israel. The Psalms of David are full of this description of God, and the 23rd Psalm, which we still use on every possible occasion, is only one particular example. The prophets take up the same theme. Jeremiah and Ezekiel speak of the false shepherds of their day and declare that God will himself be the true shepherd of his people. Isaiah takes up the same image: 'He shall feed his flock like a shepherd'; so the good shepherd, the owner of the flock and not the hired labourer, meant either God himself or his anointed one. We may well, when we listen to Crimond being sung well come away saying, 'Wasn't that lovely?' Nothing is more certain than that, when Jesus said, 'I am the good shepherd', they would come away saying: 'That was blasphemy. Who does he think he is?' For they would have recognized, without a shadow of a doubt, the enormous claim being made.

2 *Application of the image*

Although today's Gospel passage is about Jesus, it has been, of course, applied more widely. From New Testament times the concepts of shepherd and flock have been used to describe the relationship of Christian clergy to their congregations. It is the pastoral work of the clergy that tends to be most emphasized today, sometimes to the detriment of their prophetic or priestly role.

But the application is wider still, for a Christian congregation shares in the pastoral ministry of the Church. If we are concerned about other people as individuals, the pastoral element is bound to come in, so what is it that this passage has to say to us about our caring, our concern, our love for other people? Its first words are words of warning. It talks about hirelings, about those who are in it for the money or whatever else they can get out of it. We may not think that these warnings are very relevant to us. In the ranks of the ordained ministry the time has long passed when people went into that work for the money or a social rise and, indeed, for any real security. I recall with great clarity, when the news of my vocation was communicated to a family friend, that the comment was made, 'Well you won't be out of a job'; but there *are* now clergy out of a job and, indeed, on the dole.

We come back to the rest of us and the pastoral opportunities that we take. 'Whatever made up our motives, gain is surely not one of them', we would say, but we have to be careful about this. We remember first of all what is implied by 'do-goodery'—the feeling of self-satisfaction that comes from putting ourselves out; or the pleasure that we can derive by being just a bit of a busybody; or (looking at a more subtle motive), we can need to be needed. The help that we may give to others in some kind of need, may be an expression of our own. It can make us, quite unconsciously, want to keep people in some permanent state of dependence upon us.

3 The quality of God's authority

The Gospel speaks in terms of black and white, but we think in various shades of grey. We see this when we turn to the witness of him who is described as the good shepherd. In the Old Testament the word referred very often to a ruler, and the reference in our text is to the kind of authority which Jesus has over us. That is why the adjective 'good' is used. It is not to the reality of Jesus' rule that the evangelist directs us but to its quality, and the outstanding feature of its character is sacrifice. He is the one who lays down his life for the sheep. It may be said, 'Did Jesus really want nothing for himself?' The recurring theme of the Bible is that God's love is seeking the love of men and women, and we cannot imagine any form of love that does not in some way want love. The essence of love is surely that it is returned; yet the love that God seeks is the free response of adults. In our human love we often try to mould people into what we think they should be; indeed, what in some way suits us. But God, the creator of infinite variety, rejoices in the diversity of his creation.

Conclusion

So then, the good shepherd always stands in some kind of judgment upon us. His whiteness shows up our greyness, but the very word, shepherd, shows us that there is more to it than that. It shows us that he loves us and cares for us. God help us to be what we were meant to be, for after judgment comes moderation, and after forgiveness new power.

EASTER 3

The Easter question

John 11.25 *'I am the resurrection and I am life.'*

Those of us, who do jigsaw puzzles or attempt the more difficult crosswords, have often found that one particular piece or word opens the way to completing the puzzle or the crossword, and until we find this piece or this word we are held up. Something like this is true in religious matters. When you are faced with a particular religious problem you often find that, when you have found the answer to one particular question, you have found the answer to many others. The difficulty is that sometimes we ask the wrong questions, and sometimes, even if we ask the right questions, we get the wrong answers.

1 *The wrong question*

This is particularly true of the resurrection of Jesus. Many of us, when we are faced with the words in the Creed, 'And the third day he rose again from the dead,' tend to ask such questions as, 'What really happened on the first Easter Day?' 'Did Jesus really show himself alive?' And in order to answer these questions we study the Bible and find that the stories are perplexing and do not give us very clear answers, partly because they are written from different standpoints and emphasize different aspects.

The fact of the matter is that, when we ask such questions, we are asking the wrong questions first. We can only ask and try to answer such questions when we have first answered a much more fundamental one, and this is it. Who was this person who is said to have risen again and shown himself alive after death to his friends? Upon our answer to this question will depend the answers to these other questions.

Who then was Jesus? Let us suppose we say Jesus was a remarkable human being who lived in the first century and was a gifted healer and preacher and was put to death as a criminal by his enemies. Now this is a true statement as far as it goes, but it only goes so far as to rank Jesus among other remarkable human beings, of whom there have been many in different spheres of life and achievement. If this is all we can say about Jesus, then we shall naturally go on to say that the resurrection is just a pious story put out by his friends and that the tomb was not really empty on the first Easter Day. No one has ever heard of a human being, however remarkable, coming to life again, so why should it have happened in the case of Jesus? We have here asked the right question, but from the Christian point of view we have given the wrong answer, and the resurrection and the empty tomb are dismissed as meaningless.

2 The right question

Who then was Jesus? Let us suppose we say, as Christians have always said, that he was more than a remarkable human being, and add that he was also God in human form on earth.

To say this is to say that such a tremendous miracle has occurred that all other miracles, including the resurrection, pale into insignificance beside it. This is how an ancient writer put it many years ago: 'He, who so loved the world that for our sakes he was made in time; through whom all times were made; was made man who made man; was created of a mother whom he created; was carried by hands which he formed; cried in the manger in wordless infancy; he the word without whom all human eloquence is muted.'

The fact is that if we really believe that God came to earth at Christmas, then the resurrection and the empty tomb seem thoroughly appropriate and suitable. As Peter said in his great sermon recorded in the Acts of the Apostles, 'God raised him to life again, setting him free from the pangs of death, because it could not be that death should keep him in its grip.' (Acts 2.24)

It is only when we start saying the right things about

91

Jesus that all that happened at Easter begins to make sense. That is the reason why Jesus showed himself alive after Good Friday only to those who had already begun to ask the right questions about him and given the right answers. He did not show himself to Pontius Pilate or Herod or Caiaphas or other unbelievers. There was not much point because they had not even started to ask the right questions, much less give the right answers.

EASTER 4

The supreme need

> John 14.8 *Philip said, 'Lord, show us the Father and we ask no more.'*

1 *The need aroused*

Philip's request surprised Jesus and this fact surprises us. Why should Jesus have expected his disciples to have understood the real nature of his life and his character so soon? At this stage they had only known him a couple of years at the most. It is true that he had said some supportive things and performed a number of external acts. It is true that he was a most lovable person and had won their deep loyalty, but were these enough to have aroused this amazing expectation? Could these things be expected to have led the disciples to have known that, in looking upon Jesus, they were, in fact, looking upon God?

The truth is that Jesus was himself becoming increasingly aware of his unique character, and this at a time when he was becoming less popular with his contemporaries. No doubt, this partly accounts for his great joy when Peter at Caesarea Philippi showed great perception in seeing what Jesus' role really was. 'Flesh and blood has not shown this to you but my Father in Heaven.' But Philip's question has a value all of its own. 'Show us the

Father,' he says, and it is still man's deepest need to know the Father.

This, after all, is why the disciples had gone with Jesus in the first place. They believed that he was in communion with the Father and that they could, therefore, learn much from him, so they left home and family. They gave up their jobs and they risked the future. They thought that here might be that pearl of great price, for which one sacrifices everything.

So this prompts Philip's request, 'Show us the Father.' William Temple in his great commentary on St John's Gospel says, 'This is the craving which alone causes restlessness. If that be satisfied all desire is quiet. It is much to learn that this is our one great need.' This is what the disciples had learned. Whatever else we may feel about these ordinary men who followed Jesus, this stands to their credit at all times. They were men who had learned the supreme need of man to know God.

2 The need deepened

Of course, there is hidden in this request a deeper fact. Philip had been long enough with Jesus to have learned that the God, for whom his heart craved, was not the traditional God of the Jews. When he asked, 'Show us the Father,' that at least he had learned from Jesus. It was Jesus who had taught them that God was their Father, and they were at least sure about that now. It was an assurance vastly different from asking to be assured of the existence of God. What Philip seems to be saying is, 'We believe in God; now show us the Father.'

Jesus replies in a claim likely to take anyone's breath away. 'He that has seen me has seen the Father.' There can be no possible compromise about this statement of Jesus. Jesus is saying, 'I am God. To know me is to know God.' This emphasizes that there can be no possible halfway house. Either what Jesus is saying is true or he is deluded. If it is true, the rest of all the religions of the world are cut down to human size at a stroke, for there is nowhere any suggestion of any other great religious leader in the world (and there have been many), claiming to be part of the Godhead itself.

3 *The need met*

Twenty centuries of closest study and analysis of the character of Jesus seem only to confirm his claim. The more we have come to know Jesus, the clearer has become our picture of what God is like, and at the centre of that picture is the Father. The divine character, which emerges as the years roll by, is not so much that of creator, sustainer, artificer, although all those are there, but of the Father. Occasionally we may go into a cathedral or parish church, which has a lovely roof. In order to help us look at the beauty above us, a large mirror may be placed in the nave, in which is reflected that roof in all its glory, and through that mirror it can be fully appreciated. Christ tells us that he is the mirror of the Father. As we see him moving about Palestine, uttering his striking sayings, performing his healing actions, bringing peace in word and deed, we are looking into the heart of the Father.

Application

There is a warning in this incident that ought not to be overlooked. Jesus said, 'Have I been with you such a long time and yet you have not really understood me?' If after these few brief months Jesus expected his disciples to have so advanced a view of him and to recognize the Father in him, what does he expect of us, many of whom have known him from childhood into old age? It is worth asking, 'How much better do I know Jesus today than ten years ago?' In saying that, it does not mean that our views will change fundamentally, but will be enriched. In the realm of music we do not add new notes to the scale, but that does not prevent musical progress. It begins it. Out of the fixed scale came the symphonies of Beethoven, and others yet to be born will come from it. In the realm of religion we believe that Jesus is the moral and spiritual ultimate. We have a fixed point, but the point is not fixed. Jesus is not behind us in the past. He is our great contemporary, and more than that he is ahead of us calling us into a new life.

Far too many are too content with the vision of Jesus which belonged to childhood. Childlike we should all seek to be, but many of us indulge in perpetual childishness. That, as far as our vision of Christ is concerned, is deadly. Philip, advanced though he was, failed to make the most of the vision that had come to him, and Christ rebuked him for it. So the challenge is that we should so love Christ as to make the most of the revelation given to us.

EASTER 5

Intercessory prayer

John 16.24 *'Ask and you will receive.'*

1 *The problem*

'Dear Rector, We were glad to see you last week, but God has let me down. My mother has died of cancer and he didn't help her; and don't say, I should have prayed. I did and it didn't help.'

This is part of a genuine letter written by a teenage girl, who had to try and cope with her mother through all the pain and distress of a particularly unpleasant form of terminal cancer. She frequently attended church, prayed to God and seemed to get no answer. Yet we are told, 'Ask and you will receive.' Does this mean that we should not really ask in spite of what the Bible says? Of course, it does nothing of the kind. In his great book of prayer, *Becoming what I am*, Harry Williams says: 'There is a certain childlike truthfulness in asking. It is natural and we should do it.'

But what is the point if it does not work? An American church put up a notice saying, 'God loves you and so does the vicar.' It was easy to test the claim about the vicar. Was he truly helpful to those in need? Did he put himself out for others in prayer and action? We soon know whether or not a *person* really loves us; but what about *God*? It is easy to quote text after text about God's love for us, but do they repeat anything more than polite jargon? Can we blame that young girl for thinking that God did not love her or her mother? After all, she played her part. She went to church and she prayed!

2 *The answer*

In a moving and at times amusing book, *Children's letters to God*, there is one which goes, 'Dear God, If you will make it so that I can be invisible when I want to, I will do all the things you want. Is it a deal? Your friend, Gordon.' I happen to prefer:

> 'What He came on earth to do,
> And the answer that came to the prayers that He prayed,
> Were His power to see it through.'

How natural of that young girl to pray to God to make her mother better. Of course, it is the kind of *asking* prayer that we all make from time to time. But if we are to follow the example of Jesus, then our prayer must always also be, 'Thy will be done', a phrase both from the Lord's Prayer and from our Lord's agony in the garden of Gethsemane before his arrest and crucifixion. The answer for the person suffering from cancer or the man facing disaster will be the same answer given to Jesus, as he prayed for power to see it through.

Recently I called on a lady very well known to me, whom I knew to have cancer of the liver. She met me at the door and said, 'I have got liver cancer, you know,' and proceeded to say that she had this ·information from the rather co-operative young man who had been her consultant. She went on to say, 'I have always loved journeys,' as indeed she had, for she had been with me to the Holy Land, to Greece, to Rome and to Iona. 'This,' she said, 'will be the most exciting journey of all, and when I get there, Charles will say, "What kept you so long?"' (Charles, her husband, had died fifteen years before). I was deeply moved; but I realized—and have gone on to realize beyond her death (which came two months later)—that here was a truly Christian outlook. She had been given, through her faith, the power to see it through, and all fear was removed. She died gloriously, shortly after receiving the blessed sacrament, and I have not the slightest doubt that she will attain the peace, for which all hearts do strive.

3 The ministry of failures

Because this is a world in which there is evil, we have to face in life suffering and sadness and many disappointments. I have been thinking of the story of the death of Moses. Moses, with whom God talked face to face, going up into the mountain and viewing the promised land. He had led his people through the weary years of the wilderness wandering, with all the trials and tribulations inevitable in the leadership of the people. We think of the mutterings and murmurings, the wild worship of the golden calf and the burden of judging the people, and now from Mount Nebo he is allowed to view the country with all its richness and beauty, promised to his people and into which they are to go, but he is told that, while he may gaze upon it from afar, he is never to enter it himself.

This story somehow seems to epitomize that element in life, which so often brings us disappointments and failures. Sometimes it may be through our own fault, our own weakness and our disobedience, but often this is not the case. We feel we are victims of circumstances over which we have small control, and we learn that life is uncertain and transitory. Painful and distressing as it is, we have to accept this uncertain element of disappointment in life and face bravely its implications. What makes the difference for us is that we know we are in the hands of a God who is working out a love purpose, who cares for us as his dear children and who, in Christ, calls us to co-operate with him.

I suppose that one of my favourite texts in the Old Testament is, 'Even as an eagle stirs up her nest, so the Lord did lead them.' The eagle stirred up her nest in order to make the young ones fly. Otherwise, they were so comfortable that they would never have left. But the act of flying made them eagles; and the act of living, facing disappointments and dangers, enables us to grow in character.

Conclusion

In a sense, therefore, we must not trouble ourselves too much about answers to prayer. What matters is that we persevere, that we go on trying in the face of any feeling of discouragement and difficulty, because the fact that we *do* pray is a sure sign that God is at work in us. God always hears our prayers and answers them, although (and this is hard to take on occasion) if we have asked properly in Christ's name and the answer is not as we wish, we have to understand that there are times when God says, 'No!' The great poet, A. E. Housman, in an exquisite poem, writes of 'The loveliest of trees, the cherry, hung with bloom, wearing white for Eastertide', and he laments the shortness of the allotted span of life, which will leave him only a limited number of years to 'go about the woodlands' and 'to see the cherry hung with snow.' The truth is otherwise. In heaven, we shall be gazing on all that is lovely and beautiful.

When we are saddened by life's disappointments we need to remember that they also have a good side. The fault with most of us is that we are too obsessed with the things of this life. If we received all the satisfaction that we wanted in the furtherance of this life, we should become even more lodged in this world and ignore the fact that the goal before us is the vision of God. The disappointments, which we must face in life, point us surely to something far more wonderful, which is to come, to the fulfilment of man's eternal destiny. The best is yet to be!

THE SUNDAY AFTER
ASCENSION DAY

The life beyond

Luke 24.46 *'The Messiah is to suffer death and to rise from the dead on the third day.'*

One of the questions I am most frequently asked by all kinds of people, whether regular churchgoers or not, is: 'Do we really know anything about life after death?' In trying to answer this, I do not pretend to be able to say anything new or startling and certainly not to deal in any way with the debatable question of communication with those who have died, because Christianity says very little that is tangible on this matter. Furthermore, although some well-known scientists believe in it and value it, such attempts have great dangers, which will make ordinary folk leave well alone.

1 *Resurrection, not survival*

At the outset it must be made plain that the Christian idea of the resurrection is very much more than mere survival. If you believe in Christianity at all, you have to believe in a future life; otherwise, the life and death and resurrection of Jesus Christ have no meaning. God is love; he calls us his children and he loves us while we are here. It is inconceivable that death should bring his loved ones to an end. Jesus said, 'I come to prepare a place for you,' and to the thief on the cross, 'Today you shall be with me in Paradise.' So Jesus is talking about two personalities together in the future life; and the very word, 'today' helps us to realize that we do not sleep for ages, awaiting resurrection. The whole question of time is a relative matter, and it has truly been said that death is only a bend in the road of life. What the Christian has to understand is that death is the gateway to a new life and not to an agelong sleep; that though our bodies may be laid in the grave, our personalities—our

99

true selves—enter a new kind of life. When visits are made to a grave, we have to recognize that our Lord is standing outside and saying, 'He that believes in me shall never die.'

St Paul says what we shall be like. He says, 'There is a natural body and there is a spiritual body.' The natural body we know; the spiritual we cannot describe. Our Lord, when refuting the Sadducees' question about the resurrection, said, 'They are like angels in heaven,' in a picture language which they could understand. After the resurrection our Lord himself appears in a spiritual body, which makes us believe that the body has a form similar to our present body, by which recognition is possible.

2 *Activity and growth in the life beyond*

At one time our churches were full of paintings encouraged by picture and symbolic verse about how we would be occupying our time in a future life. Men and women were shown playing harps and singing in choirs or sitting by streams in Elysian fields. These pictures, which, to do their authors justice, were figurative and not meant to be taken literally, made the future life appear a thoroughly boring existence. But our Lord suggests in the parable of the talents that the reward for service here will be further service in the life beyond. Love fulfils itself in service; and rest, as shown in the future life, can be taken as in the line of one of our hymns, 'In perfect work shall be perfect rest.'

Again, the Christian faith implies that there must be growth in our characters in the life beyond; although our aim here is perfection, no one reaches it here. I cannot see that the process of death is going to make any difference to our personalities. We are not perfect when we die, and perfection is God's purpose for us. So it is clear that there must be growth and that, as we are given a more perfect perception of what God's love and purpose is, we shall grow into the stature of the fullness of Christ.

3 Judgement and the life beyond

What about the question of rewards and punishment, of which we read in the New Testament? There can be little doubt that Christ taught that this life is a preparation for the next. However much we may revolt against the material pictures of hell (and rightly so), yet there can be little doubt that Christ speaks of a future judgement for all, especially for those who have deliberately refused to live according to the light that has been given to them. We are told that our Lord himself, who knows what is in man, his difficulties and his trials, will be the judge who is merciful and very kind. I doubt if all the pictures of a material hellfire would be as bad as looking into those eyes of love, when we have deliberately rejected him and the highest that is in us, and we realize that he knows the flimsiness of our excuses. Once more, Christianity teaches that in the future life we shall be able to comprehend the beauty, the wonder and the love of God himself. Now we know a part of it, but then we shall know the whole.

All these things say to us that, because of the resurrection of Christ, death is certainly not the end of us, though it is of our natural body. It is the entrance for our personality to a new and fuller life with a spiritual body, through which recognition will be possible of those we love in the family of God. We enter that life with the same character and personality with which we leave this one. We shall not remain static but be given a chance to grow towards perfection. As we have tried to be faithful here to what is highest, God will give us further service in the life to come. In this higher fellowship God the Father will show himself to us, and we shall know what love really means.

4 Two golden rules for this life

In all this, for you and me there are two most important messages. First, the thought of the future life should keep us young in mind. This life is so small a proportion of life as a whole, that it should make us continually eager to learn to be ready for fresh wonder. Secondly, it should brace us for new effort. We do not wish to go to that life shrivelled and useless personalities, who have learnt nothing but self-gratification, but strong virile souls, who have done our bit to work out the eternal purposes of God through serving our generation with his help. God knows we made many mistakes and even failed miserably; but if this has been our motive and we show something of the Christlike spirit in our relation to others in reliance on him day by day, he will see amongst the dross something of himself, and it will enable him at the last to make us grow into his likeness, into the measure of the stature of the fullness of Christ.

PENTECOST

The Spirit comes to the Church

John 20.22 *'Receive the Holy Spirit.'*

In any teaching I undertake for Confirmation candidates, in schools and in the pulpit I find people fascinated by the Church's calendar, and especially by the first half of it. I sometimes try out a kind of public opinion poll about the Christian faith when people come to see me about a baptism or a wedding. Most of the questions are as simple as: 'Do you know what Christmas is about?' To that kind of question the answer is usually quickly and correctly given, but when one comes to a question about Lent, Good Friday and Easter Day, and the questions get further from our Lord's childhood and Christmas, then the answers become more vague and are progressively more uninformed. Lent is the time when some people give up cigarettes and sweets. Good Friday is something to do with hot cross buns. Easter is dominated by curious ideas about eggs; Whitsun was (but no longer is) a bank holiday week-end. Most people's knowledge of Christianity appears to end somewhere about verse 5 of the Sermon on the Mount.

The story of the baby Jesus and such bits as the birds of the air and the lilies of the field often seem to be the sum total of British Christian knowledge outside the worshipping Churches.

1 *Maximum impact*

If you want to find out the point at which genuine Christianity made the maximum impact upon the human race, you can do no better than to make a character study of the twelve apostles *before* the first Whit Sunday and then *after* the first Whit Sunday. The evidence about the apostles *before* that day you will find mostly in the four Gospels of Matthew, Mark, Luke and John. Before you progressed very far you would discover that the original apostolic dozen were a highly diverse group of friends.

When Jesus displayed monumental courage in the face of adversity the disciples made off. When Jesus showed patience and forbearance to the hundreds of followers who wanted his help the disciples said, 'Get rid of them.' Only a few days before his arrest Jesus found them all quarrelling about seniority and who were to have the top jobs. They seem to have misunderstood almost everything that Jesus taught them, and the apostles in the Gospels are not very attractive.

The evidence for what they were like *after* the first Whit Sunday is to be found mainly in the Acts of the Apostles, particularly in chapter 2 and the following ones. The contrast of before with after is simply staggering, and the changeover is beyond the power of simple words to tell. Before the first Whitsun the disciples had repeatedly attempted to imitate the character of Jesus and they had failed. Afterwards they found for the first time that their tentative efforts to imitate the character of Jesus were now beginning to succeed.

No honest reader of the New Testament can evade the conclusion that something very powerful and very unusual has happened. People are unquestionably being changed at the root of their being. Cowards become

103

heroes; sinners are transformed; fear, greed, envy and pride are expelled by a flood of something above and beyond normal human experience, for in the pages of the New Testament the cruel, the wicked, the evilminded and the godless become filled with selfless love and with generous courage. The critics of the Christian faith have somehow got to explain this.

Moreover, within a couple of generations the message of Christ was being taken by devoted men and women to a good part of the then known world. Consequently, it is a matter of simple historical fact that never before has any small body of ordinary people so moved the world that their enemies could say that 'these men have turned the world upside down'. (Acts 17.6)

2 *Right words*

The word, 'semantics', is a useful word. Very roughly, semantics is the art of choosing the right words to describe an event. When the event happens to be unique then the problem of semantics is a formidable one. In chapter 2 of the Acts, which describes the first Whitsun, St Luke has to strain the ability of ordinary words almost to breaking point, in order to describe what happened when the power of the Holy Spirit seized collectively upon the young Church with its then small membership. They were invested by a hitherto unknown dynamic and became, in an almost literal sense, new men.

Jesus had said long before that all this would happen. But they were too engrossed in their own importance to pay attention. Jesus had said, 'I will pray the Father and he shall give you another Comforter, that he may be with you forever,' and the Holy Spirit has done precisely that.

The Holy Spirit is the very life's breath of the Church now, and it has always been so in every one of the eighty previous generations which separate the apostles' age from our own. The Church is not a free and fossilized holy club for the rich and the senile. The Church is the most dangerous company of the young in spirit that the contemporary world contains.

When St Luke was wrestling with words in trying to write chapter 2 of the Acts, he picked on the words, 'wind' and 'fire'. These two words had to convey the huge dynamic which he was trying to reduce to plain writing, so that other men might read and understand. Wind and fire are nature's two most powerful agents, and they are both agents of cleansing as well.

At some time or another everyone is faced with a problem of semantics. This is why love letters are so moving and so descriptive, and why other people's love letters are often so excruciatingly funny. There is a passage in Pepys' Diary, 27th February 1668, when he had been to a concert. He had heard some music for the oboe and Pepys records that it was so beautiful that it made him feel 'quite sick'. What an odd way, we may feel, for so great a literary man to solve his problem of semantics, but his words were the nearest that he could get to describe the ravishment of soul and spirit that the lovely melodies brought to him.

Conclusion

How very well that skilful and sensitive writer, Luke, did with *his* semantic problem of putting into frail human words what had happened on that first Whit Sunday! Wind and fire indeed! May that wind blow clean and may that fire cheer and warm contemporary Christians now—as happened so long ago when the Church was young and the Christian faith was brand new!

TRINITY SUNDAY

Questions about worship

> John 14.15–16 *'If you love me you will obey my commands; and I will ask the Father, and he will give you another to be your Advocate, who will be with you for ever—the Spirit of truth.'*

Not long ago I was challenged by a gentleman in my parish as to why the Church did not adapt itself to the needs of the day by a use of the methods of the theatre and the cinema. He declared that a body of clergy, prepared to 'spring surprises upon a congregation', would attract many new churchgoers.

The weakness of this argument lies in its failure to realize the true meaning of worship, and this ignorance is to be observed in many otherwise educated laymen; nor is it confined to one class of society; it is widespread and deep-rooted. One finds it expressed in the words of the working woman, who declared that she had ceased to attend church because, as she said, 'I never feel any better for going.' Also, in the words of a retired stockbroker, who said that, although he disapproved of his rector's views on most subjects, he continued to attend church occasionally, because 'religion keeps one straight'.

1 *What is the Church?*

But what, after all, is the Church of God and what is its purpose in the world? It is the great society of the baptised, living and dead; it is the great society brought into being by the life, death and resurrection of Jesus Christ, a society through which the Holy Spirit of God moves and works. As our text says: 'Your Advocate, who will be with you for ever—the Spirit of truth.'

St Paul calls the Church, 'the body of Christ', meaning that as at Bethlehem the second person of the Holy Trinity took to himself a human body, by means of which to reveal himself to men; so Christ reveals himself to the world today through that body of people, whom we call the Church. The Church is 'the body of Christ', because through it the risen, ascended Saviour makes himself known to the world today. By our baptism 'we are members of Christ's body, the Church', and within that body we may, if we will, be fed with the grace of God.

It is our duty, as members of Christ's Church, to be present at its meetings in church and, in particular, at the Lord's own service. We must remember that the other services in the Book of Common Prayer were never intended to replace the Holy Communion. Historically, Matins came into existence as a service of preparation for the Holy Communion, and Evensong as a service of thanksgiving for the Holy Communion, for it is at the Holy Communion that we obey our Lord's dying command, 'Do this in remembrance of me,' and it is there that we realize our membership of the family of God. It is, therefore, hard to understand how professing Christians can fail to be present on the Lord's day at the service which Christ himself gave us.

2 Why worship?

The Church was intended by our Lord to be a family of people, united in him in the power of the Holy Spirit in the bonds of an unswerving love and obedience. The instructed Christian attends church to worship and not necessarily to be edified or amused, nor do we attend church that we may 'feel better for going'. The state of our feelings depends upon a large number of factors, such as the state of our liver, our domestic life, our food, our work and a host of other things. Nor is it sufficient excuse for those, who absent themselves from Church although claiming to be Christians, to say that, nevertheless, they are 'just as good as those who go'. This may even be all too true, because some habitual churchgoers are unpleasant people; but this again has nothing to do with our true reason for churchgoing.

107

The Church is not *primarily* an organization for maintaining good conduct—though this should be incidental; but it is a worshipping society. The word, 'worship' means 'worth-ship', and to worship means to approach God, not for what we may obtain, but that we may give him our 'bounden duty and service', for it is *that*, and that alone, that God is worth. So it is that the instructed Christian will worship, Sunday by Sunday—despite the sermon, the music, feelings afterwards, and despite even the person in the row behind!

The exhortation at Matins and Evensong reminds us that we meet in God's house first of all, 'to give thanks for the great benefits that we have received at his hands', and secondly, 'to tell forth his praise'. If we love God, our heavenly Father, it will be unthinkable for us to be absent from God's house on Sunday, and it will be the most natural thing in the world for us to be present at the altar every Lord's day. It has sometimes been noted that those who are most vocal in criticizing the services of the Church are also those who are not themselves remarkable for their regularity in Church attendance. If people do not love God, then although various stunts, if adopted, may cause them to attend Church services on occasion, all will be valueless, unless they can be brought to know God as a loving friend and Father.

3 *An optional extra?*

From time to time I have heard complaints from those serving in the forces that, whereas Roman Catholics, for example, are given every facility for attending Mass on Sundays, no such facilities are afforded members of the Church of England. While I do not wish to contest the truth or otherwise of this statement, one thing is certain. The Roman Catholic is instructed that it is a solemn duty to be present at Mass on Sundays, and to be absent without sufficient cause is a sin. We may not agree with this, although there is sound scriptural precedent for the Christian being present every Sunday to worship with his fellow

Christians. But, while some Church people continue to look upon churchgoing as an optional appendage to the Christian religion, and absent themselves from worship on the most flimsy pretext, it is hardly to be wondered at if military and other authorities are sometimes inclined to say, 'Well, attendance at church does not appear to matter for you people and, therefore, there is no particular reason why we should make arrangements for you to attend church.' Those who love God will be found regularly in his house.

PENTECOST 2

What is a Christian?

> Luke 14.15 *'Happy the man who shall sit at the feast in the kingdom of God.'*

So said the man who made what he considered a suitably pious remark, when Jesus was talking about those who deserve a place at that heavenly banquet. In our reading today he is soon cut down to size, because our Lord shows that all our excuses for half-hearted behaviour will be put under close scrutiny by God. Ask yourself again, 'What does Jesus require of us? What do we mean by a Christian?'

1 *Believing*

First, to be a Christian means to believe. The central Christian belief is that Jesus is divine, which means that he is the *perfect* image of God. If you believe he was the one perfect unselfish being who has ever lived on this earth, then you see in him an exact likeness of the unselfishness, love and goodness of God himself.

The earliest Christian creed consisted of the three words, 'Jesus is Lord'. This meant that Jesus had come to earth and lived here. The verb is important, because it implied belief in the resurrection and the ascension. The Christian believes Christ to be *alive*, not a past character in history. The word, Lord, is the key, because it means that he is master and controller. The simple creed is still central to Christian belief.

To believe in his divinity is to hold that the power behind the universe is that same selfless love as was shown in the life and death and resurrection of Christ. It is to believe that God is stronger than evil, that truth, beauty and goodness are ultimate values, that light will always overcome darkness, and that life is stronger than death.

2 *Belonging*

To be a Christian is to belong to the Church. People are apt to reject the Church. They say, 'Why can't a man be a Christian without going to Church?' But we only know about Christ because the early Church preserved and handed down records about him. The Church is the strongest proof of his resurrection and his present existence. Were it not for the Church in the past, we should never have become Christian people. It is naive to say that we do not believe in the Church. However individualistic a Christian may be, he is always in debt to the Church, not least for Baptism, Confirmation and Holy Communion, for without it they would not be possible.

Christ founded the Church to satisfy man's need of others and his craving for belonging. Of course, the Church has faults and has made many mistakes. Moreover its members are struggling and often fail, but they are at least travelling in the right direction and this is what counts in the end.

3 *Behaving*

To be a Christian means to behave in a certain way and to pursue a fixed line of conduct; which is, as the Rotarians say, 'Service before self'. Service is the rent we pay for our room on earth, and it is a constant Christian duty. Despite all that is done today by the welfare state, the task of the Christian remains. It is for him or her to take part in service for others, and to bring to that service an essential Christian characteristic of love and reverence for human personality, which is by no means too common today. Believing that every individual soul is of infinite worth indicates that people must never be treated as means, but only as ends; so this should determine the Christian attitude not only to individuals but also to nations and to races.

The Christian should have always a painful sensitivity to the wrongs of the world and try to serve our fellow men without those two disastrous tendencies—which so often turn benefactors into malefactors—the great temptation to be possessive of the people that we try to help, and the tendency to be patronizing. The Christian should be saved from both, because he should be humble enough to be deeply aware of his debt to God and to others, and of his own inadequacies and sins.

Conclusion

To sum up. To be a Christian means three things; believing, belonging and behaving. It means holding a certain belief, belonging to a certain society and behaving in a certain way—the way of service, not self. Caring is the principal characteristic, caring for God, caring for the Church and caring for others. Do you?

PENTECOST 3

A call to courageous discipline

Luke 8.50 *'Do not be afraid, only show faith.'*

1 *An example of discipline*

Some time ago I was admitting a new Enrolling Member to the Mothers' Union Branch in my parish, in the course of the Sunday Parish Communion. The Mothers' Union is one of the really great societies in the Church, and it so happens that this parish has had a branch for over one hundred years. In each of the parishes, where I have been privileged to be the incumbent, I have looked upon its members as supportive of real progress in prayer, in worship and in sheer hard work. In days of rapidly falling standards, with divorce threatening one in three of all marriages in this country and a scorning of Christian standards of morality, adult organizations within the Church, whose members do not flinch to stand four-square on the faith, are vital to us all. Time and again the Mothers' Union has pointed the whole Church to her duty. May she continue to do so!

The Mothers' Union is a disciplined handmaid of the Church, and it is discipline that we lack today. When we think of a good mother, we know just how much personal discipline of action is involved, if the family is to be held together and really cared for. A good family revolves around her. These mature disciplines the Mothers' Union has enlarged so that its members aim at regular prayer, Bible reading, attendance at the blessed sacrament and proper stewardship as part of their disciplines, too, and God only knows how much the Church owes to such godly attitudes in its members. This then is a body of Christian mothers, bound by the Christian disciplines, which should bind us all, and I remind you that they are not optional extras but the distinguishing marks of the true Christian.

When the last war started William Temple said, 'We enter the war as a dedicated nation, and it is this fact which has called forth the response of the younger generation in so marvellous a manner. The prevailing conviction is that Nazi tyranny and oppression are destroying the traditional excellences of European civilization and must be eliminated for the good of mankind. Over against the deified nation of the Nazis, our people have taken their stand as a dedicated nation.' This was not an exaggerated statement of the position. The National Days of Prayer, the Sword of the Spirit, the Malvern Conference, and much else made it clear that ordinary people were aware of the spiritual issues at stake. Yet the foundations of civilized life were being shaken.

2 *A general loss of discipline*

When the war ended in that lurid flash, which annihilated the Japanese city of Nagasaki, and the world turned to rebuilding its shattered cities and its broken homes, it gradually became clear that the price paid had exhausted the moral and spiritual capital amassed during the Christian centuries. The idealism, which sought to build moral values and spiritual insights into the educational system of this country in the 1944 Act, depended upon a supply of teachers convinced, in William Temple's words, that 'education is only adequate and worthy when it is itself religious', but there was no such supply of committed Christian teachers. The idealism of F. D. Maurice, Charles Gore and William Temple had given place to an acquisitive society, a society bent on pleasure envisaged in the crudest terms, a permissive society in which anything goes—easy sex, easy drink, easy drugs, all procurable by easy money; a society in which anything was justified to secure its own ends, a society of incredible vulgarity—of betting shops and bingo halls, of cheap pornography and strip shows, of battered babies and meths men, of football hooliganism and vandalism of public property, of contraceptives, abortion and divorce on demand, of frauds perpetuated by MPs and others in high places, and suspect honours' lists, and theatre shows sickening in their sheer vulgarity.

What has the Church been doing in these years which the locusts have eaten? Let us be totally honest about this; it has halved the number of its parish priests and doubled the number of its bishops; it has perfected its bureaucracy and produced a large number of 'specialist ministries', where there is neither altar nor pulpit to serve. It has 'reconsidered its structures', whatever they may be, and set up synods, which a previous Bishop of Southwark

113

described as stamping grounds for bores and bureaucrats. It has jettisoned the Authorized Version of the Book of Common Prayer and sought to replace them with liturgical compositions of an inferior English prose style and spiritual depth, as many believe. We have been swept away on the tide of popular opinion, and in many respects have allowed ourselves to become conformed to this world. For these things may God forgive us!

Surely we need, as a nation, to be recalled to discipline. It is indiscipline that is ruining our country. Children without discipline either at home or school can hardly be blamed if they relapse into savagery. I have been told of some clergy trained in certain theological colleges, which have ceased to inculcate the traditional disciplines of regular daily prayer based upon the Office and the Eucharist; the framework of life making provision for meditation, reading, pastoral visiting, especially of the sick and aged; of teaching both old and young, especially those being prepared for the sacraments. All this is in danger of being lost as the basis of pastoral care and evangelism.

3 *A call for a lead in discipline*

There is a great need for leaders, to help us to restore the broken-backed standards in theology, in worship and in morality. In theology we have drifted far from the strongly-held incarnational theology of Charles Gore and William Temple. Today we seem ashamed to acknowledge the uniqueness of the revelation of God's glory in Christ. Some Christian leaders seem anxious to tell us that there *are* other names under Heaven, given among men, whereby we may be saved. With all the riches of Christian spirituality at our disposal, we are being told that oriental pantheism has better forms of meditation. Any recall to religion today must begin with the conviction that the Church holds God's truth in trust for mankind. If the trumpet give an uncertain sound, who will prepare for battle?

And if there is no other foundation for our theology

114

than that which is Jesus Christ, how much more true is this of our worship? Worship is the concentration of all that we have and are upon God. The magnificence of church architecture, the glory of church music, the noble cadence of liturgical language and the solemn dignity of ceremonial, all speak to the worshippers of the otherness, the transcendence of God. May God grant that we should not be afraid to speak of these things, nor to condemn much of the shallow trendiness of what passes for worship today! Is it strange that the slovenly indifference, which characterizes so much of modern worship. should be reflected in moral chaos?

St Paul said that theological error works itself out in moral error, 'Wherefore God gave them up in the lusts of their hearts unto uncleanness that their bodies should be dishonoured among themselves. They have exchanged the truth of God for a lie, and worship and serve the creature rather than the creator, who is blessed forever.' Away then with the agonizing over the 'Church's role in contemporary society', so much questioned in so many committees set up today. This role is what it has always been—to point people to God. And in the Church of England we have a wonderful armoury to do just this. We have no cause to be ashamed of the Christian faith, nor of the Church of England, so long as she remains faithful to Scripture and catholic truth and proclaims that other foundation can no man lay than that which has been laid, which is Jesus Christ. Pray that God will give us leaders, clerical and lay, to proclaim, as Haggai in old Jerusalem when the Lord's house lay in ruins, 'Who is left among you that saw this house in its former glory; and how do you see it now? Is it not in your eyes as nothing? Now be strong, all you people of the land, saith the Lord, and work, for the latter glory of this house shall be greater than the former, and in this place will I give peace, saith the Lord of Hosts'; 'to whom be all might, majesty, dominion and power.'

PENTECOST 4

The Church's mission to the individual

Luke 15.10 *'There is joy among the angels of God over one sinner who repents.'*

Whenever we read St Luke's Gospel we are conscious of his notebooks. It is clear that pages of them have been incorporated en bloc, following no chronological order. Earlier in the Gospel St Luke has described the supper party in the house of Matthew, and in today's Gospel we have a section of teaching which has a special connection with that event.

1 *Three stories and their setting*

Prefaced by the words, 'Now the tax-gatherers and sinners were all drawing near to hear Jesus. And the Pharisees and scribes murmured, "This man receives sinners and eats with them",' this section contains the stories of the lost sheep, the lost coin and the lost son. The last of those stories, the story of the prodigal son, is not included in today's Gospel, but the three stories are always to be taken together. It is much to be desired, therefore, that those who take this morning's sermon seriously, shall go home and read again in its entirety this wonderful fifteenth chapter of St Luke's Gospel. It has been suggested that these three stories were incorporated into the text of a speech delivered after the supper in Matthew's house, and they probably give us as good a report of our Lord's style as we possess.

The report of these three parables is beautifully done. A thoroughly competent person would have done it at first hand. The supper in Matthew's house gave the great set-back to the smooth progress of our Lord's ministry. Jesus never recovered the caste that he lost over it in the eyes of respectable people. The upset of the elder brother seems to show us our Lord's first attempt to woo back the really good people, who were offended by the line he was taking, before the hostility of the Pharisees achieved complete possession of them. It reflects the tenderness of our Lord's treatment of the good people, who really did not understand how a good man could love publicans and sinners. The supper was probably a farewell banquet to the staff of the customhouse. Onlookers were always admitted to the house on such occasions, and some of the strict party may very well have been onlookers.

2 *Three lessons from the stories*

(a) The story of the lost sheep dwells on God's unwearying search for the sinner inspired by pity. That is all. It speaks of no other aspect of the matter. To get from it what it has to say to you, you must think of the unrelenting laws which govern us, and then again you must let Jesus Christ assure you that behind those laws is one who cares for you and for me, as we care for straying sheep on dangerous cliffs.

(b) The story of the lost coin dwells solely on the value of the sinner to God. We are not merely beings over whom God watches anxiously through a feeling of compassion. We are personally very valuable to him—one of his jewels. Our Lord makes a peasant woman the centre of this tale, because coins to an Eastern peasant woman are not only of trade value; they are her ornaments. She wears them round her head, and if a silver piece is lost her jewellery has become defective. I am valuable to God; and, more than this, God needs me for his design.

(c) We see in the third story a young man who has made an ass of himself, because he feels himself to be incapable of acting upon a perfectly pure motive. He feels that to embark on the adventure towards God with mixed motives is to be a hypocrite. Our Lord's advice to him is, 'Do not wait to make a move until you can make it from the highest motive. Make use of whatever motive you can to start in the right direction.' The prodigal son wanted the sort of board and lodging his father could give him and

117

which he could not get among the pigs. So he says, 'I will go home and admit my bad conduct and get my father to give me a job.' As he persevered with the journey back, insensibly his attitude began to change, and there came a moment, while he was still some way from home, when sonship began to rise in him again and his father from a long way off saw it. Then the two quickly got rid of the remaining distance which separated them, for our Lord switches our thoughts away from the broken boy on to the father's love. So often it makes a world of difference if we can all realize that, before the dawn breaks, the father has been watching the road.

3 *The true relationship of God and man*

It is a drawback to these stories that they are so beautiful. They seem almost too good to be true, and too charming to be scientific. Our Lord insists that not only are they scientific but that he is the scientific expert in this matter. He has to convince us that the highest personal contact known to man—the contact of the perfect father with the perfect child—most nearly approximates to the relationship which God has designed for man; but before he can put man in the right place in this matter, he has to show that in comparison with God he only has the proportion of a stray lamb or a lost coin. It is after man has accepted these comparisons that he can be humble enough to consider his relationship with God as that of son with father, and can grasp the fact that the first move is with God; and that *he* is a lost son whom God has come to find. By making the first two analogies the lost sheep and the lost coin, things with no power of responsive initiative, our Lord shows that repentance, the movement of a faulty man back to God, is first of all a movement of the love of God. It is *God*, and not the sinner, who moves first in the matter. If man seeks God, it always means that God has been seeking man. The human side comes in, 'I will arise and go to my father,' in the third story; but the pressure of God's love comes first, though man has something to do in the matter

118

also. The effort required in man's response is the traverse of a long road until, towards the end, the welcoming figure of the father comes in sight.

PENTECOST 5

Wanted—People who recognize God's Will

Luke 10.2 *'The crop is heavy, but labourers are scarce.'*

A very great man, whose name most people are unlikely to know, but whose influence has been felt a great deal in present-day writing, is de Caussade. Archbishop William Temple and Evelyn Underhill, to quote but two great Anglicans, owe much to him. De Caussade's great work, parts of which have been reproduced in a paperback recently, is called, *Abandonment to Divine Providence*. As we look at the Church's mission to the world, it is important that we should know what he has to say.

1 *Two fundamentals*

Briefly we can sum up what he writes in two sentences. First, there is *nothing*, however small or apparently indifferent, which has not been allowed by God to happen—even to the fall of the leaf. This is a tremendous statement. Everything that happens is ordained or permitted by God.

Secondly, since this is so, we must abandon ourselves to him and accept all that happens as his will for us. This is not easy, but it is commonsense. So he writes, 'All we have to do is to accept the will of God as it is known to us, moment by moment, in the guise of a duty to be done, a trial to be borne, a joy to be received; in every experience of life, without exception, God comes to us; if we receive him humbly we can and will do his will.' This he called his

119

doctrine of the 'Sacrament of the Present Moment'. The word, sacrament, means 'God hidden in matter'; and de Caussade was saying, therefore, that in every experience of our life God speaks to us, though we may not recognize it. We may resent our pain, or we may use it. We may strive against our environment, or we may accept and use it. We may say, 'If only I could work with Christians; if only my health were better; if only I had not taken so and so's advice', but, in all our circumstances, God speaks to us. This is the sacrament of the present moment, if we accept our circumstances as such. So, although one lives in perpetual doubt and ignorance about what God's will is *going* to be, we have no doubt what it *is* at this particular moment; that we always know, because *it is*, and we take every experience and see it to be sacramental, God revealing himself to us.

2 *A changed attitude*

(a) To people
It is not easy. It is not easy to see all the people, with whom we come into touch, in that way. Some of them anger us; some bore us; some we shrink from. To feel that they are all children of God is not easy, and yet we must love them. G. K. Chesterton wrote, 'Unless we love a thing in all its ugliness, we cannot make it beautiful'; and we shall only bring ourselves to love them when we pray for them. William Law, whose classic book, *A Serious Call to a Devout and Holy Life* (also now in paperback) shows how intercession 'amends and reforms the hearts of those who use it' and describes the change that constant prayer for his people brought about in Ouranius, the village priest. No doubt his pleading for them affected them, but the first thing that it did was to change his attitude to them. Christians have to learn to see God in all his creatures, to realize that in the hospital of the great Physician there are no incurable cases; and this we shall do only if our lives are rooted in prayer. Surely this was the secret of our Lord's concern for the publicans and sinners, the harlots and

brigands, and all the social outcasts of his day. Those, from whom we shrink, he loved and loves, because their estrangement hurt him the more, for he knew the image in which they were created.

(b) To chores
It is difficult enough to see people as God's children. What about the daily arduous, tiring, routine jobs that absorb our energies day by day? How hard it is to see that all these things are God's will for us and to accept him as sacramentally present in the duties of the kitchen, the answering of letters, the people we meet in the street, the filling-in of forms, the scraping of potatoes, the 'toughs' in the youth club; how hard it is to accept minor trials and tribulations and to turn them into patient acts of love towards God. It is hard; but if we pray, then these, too, can be occasions of prayer. St Francis hallowed every simple action of every day with prayer. As he picked up a piece of paper with writing on it, he would say to himself as he did so, 'This is the word of God.' As he opened his door he would say, 'Thou art the door.' As he lighted a candle, 'Thou art the light of the world.' If we could make every occasion of every day special to us in that way, then prayer would be so mixed with life that they would be one and the same thing. Finding him in every person who comes across our path, in every experience, will gradually impart to such lives a strange, unconscious power and they will be useful to God.

(c) To suffering
We can apply this doctrine of de Caussade's to many other phases of life—to the problem of pain and to the vital problem of vocation at work. Suffering, whether physical or mental, makes or breaks us, according to the way in which we accept it—with resignation and trust or with resentment and cross-querying. Von Hügel has said that Christianity 'does not explain suffering, but it does show us what to do with it.' There is a short prayer full of

121

meaning, 'Lord, for thy great pain, have mercy on my little pain.'

(d) To work

Of the problem of vocation in our work there is something to be said. One of the major issues facing the Church today is that millions of people are bored to tears by the work which earns them their daily bread. It is difficult to see how much of the work itself can be anything but tedious, but for those, who have the love of God in their hearts, it could be a great opportunity for winning souls to God. If, where there are souls, God is sacramentally present, we can use any environment, however distasteful, as a means of doing him honour. Evelyn Underhill has written, 'It is not Christian to try and get out of our frame or separate our outward life from our life of prayer, since both are the creation of one charity. The third-rate little town in the hills, with its limited social contacts and monotonous manual work, reproves us when we begin to fuss about our opportunities and our scope.'

3 *The starting point*

Our starting point is that the purpose of the spiritual life is that we should be useful to God. The cross points the way, showing us the way of self-obliteration, the way of absorption in Christ. It is Almighty God's plan that the world should see Christ in us or not see him at all. That is an appalling fact; and the world will see Christ in us only if there is the cross in our lives. What this must mean for each one of us only we can say, we and the Holy Spirit. It may mean a decision, from which we shrink back in fear. It may mean hurting those we love, because of a higher loyalty. It may mean the breaking of a friendship or the putting of it on a different level. It may mean many things; but, only if we are obedient to the voice of truth and conscience, as we see it, step by step, will the world see Christ in us.

When they do see this, mighty things begin to happen.

122

The fruit of the Spirit, love, peace, joy, will appear in our lives and we shall be useful to God, proclaiming mercy to those burdened with guilt, peace and power to those stricken with fear, healing to the sick in spirit, zeal to the tired, hope to the cynical. How immensely worth while, therefore, it all is. We see all around us the tragedy of people, to whom life is the struggle to run away from countless fears, and we dare not waste and squander the greatest of God's good gifts, which is time. So we place ourselves at the foot of the cross, that we may rise with him and share with him in the bringing of a new life into the dead bones. God grant us, therefore, broken and contrite hearts and with them a hunger and thirst for the things of the spirit and for the souls of men!

PENTECOST 6

Thoughts and advice on suffering

Mark 10.50 *'Take heart; stand up; he is calling you.'*

I always find this story of the healing of the blind young Bartimaeus a deeply moving one; partly, I suppose, it is because one of my greatest friends was a blind organist, who was my partner (if one may put it that way) whilst I was for ten years a country rector. All his music he learnt from braille sent out weekly by the National Association for the Blind. He controlled a large choir including twenty-four boys, of which my own four sons were a part, and the love and affection that he inspired amongst them will never be forgotten. Partly also, I suppose, I recall speaking to 150 children at a Harvest Thanksgiving in what was called a Sunshine Babies' Home. It was a lovely service, as such services are, but every one of those children was blind. 'The new man will see,' this lovely story tells us, and when we find ourselves asking the question, 'Does God care?', this is indeed a story to think about.

1 *The problem of suffering*

Take the question which is asked constantly of a parish priest: 'Why should this happen to me?' Now the real question is: 'Why should this happen to anyone?' The real problem to look into is not the problem of *my* pain or *my* misfortune. The problem is the same one that thousands of others are facing, too. This leads straight to the question of rewards and punishments. It is a terribly difficult question, and frankly we cannot say that rewards and punishments have anything to do with our own suffering. That would be about as far from the truth as if we said that we all got what we deserve, no more and no less. Both extremes must be ruled out. As a matter of experience, there are moments when we feel as if in some mysterious way wrongdoing has something to do with it. There *are* instances where people suffer through their own wrong-doing, of course, but there are so many people who do wrong without suffering for it (at least so far as we can tell), and there are certainly many people who suffer from other people's sins (as, I am afraid, many of the children at that Harvest Festival service, that I have spoken of, did). It seems that we have to think of other people's suffering as well as our own, if we are going to find any answer.

I feel that the whole question of rewards and punishments ties up with the condition of human nature. It is quite natural to ask the question, 'Why does God send suffering?', but it always seems to be rather beside the point. It may well be that the right answer to that question is that God doesn't send it, though he could *use* it. We don't like to be told so, but the trouble is that human nature has more to do with it than we care to admit. We all know that human nature is not perfect, but it isn't simply that. It is the fact that there is something positively wrong with human nature, and while that is the case, life just cannot work out in the way that God desires for us. If that is the case, then there is bound to be suffering. We have to remember also that this fallen human nature belongs to us all, and we can go a step further and say that we all have a hand in human suffering, directly or indirectly.

Think of it in this way. I believe that God means every-thing he made to be perfect, including human nature, which is perhaps the most wonderful thing of all that he made. Now human nature means body, mind and spirit. I believe there was a time when man was perfect in that way, but he is not perfect now. He has, as we see, fallen away from that, so this imperfection would show itself in all three parts of men's nature; and this is just what we do find. We find there are disorders and weaknesses and dis-eases in our bodies, in our minds and in our spirits, which we cannot account for in any other way. It seems to me that it isn't that God sends it; it crops up because of our human imperfection.

2 *Three pieces of advice*

(a) Avoid self-pity

I am quite sure that in the whole realm of personal suffer-ing there is one thing that we must mark down at the outset, and that is self-pity. I never heard my organist friend complain about his blindness, and indeed he was one of the happiest people I have ever known. It is terribly easy to look at other people, who seem to be in happier circumstances, and then to compare their lot with our own; and if we do this, before we know what is happen-ing, we are feeling sorry for ourselves. Once that happens, we have to fight our way out of it, unless we are going to carry a grudge against life and even against God. Whilst there are few people who really have a grudge against life in that way, there are many who have to fight against self-pity.

(b) See suffering in proportion

So we think about human suffering as we see it in other people, and this has a way of keeping things in proportion. If we see our own little bit of suffering as a tiny part of *all* human suffering, we don't forget that there are different kinds of suffering and that many of the troubles, that are hardest to bear, are those which nobody else knows much about. If only we could see into the minds of other people, we should often find that those, who appear outwardly carefree, may really be going through a great deal of mental and spiritual suffering, which they don't talk about.

(c) Sufficient unto the day

On the other hand, we are not called upon to carry this great weight of suffering all at once or by ourselves. I often think of the story of the stupid boy and his master. The boy had been told to carry a great bundle of sticks from the ditch to the farmhouse. He looked at the bundle and bent down to try and lift it, but it was too heavy for him. So the stupid boy knelt down and untied it and took a few sticks at a time. He had nearly finished the job when his master came by. Seeing the sticks left at the side of the ditch, he demanded to know what use a faggot would be all untied. The stupid boy answered, 'The only way I could carry it was to take a few sticks at a time, but they will be tied up again when I get them all home.' He was never called a stupid boy after that. I like to think of that story because it helps us to remember that we are not called to carry the whole load at once. Jesus said, 'Each day has troubles enough of its own.'

3 *An appeal*

What an opportunity this opens up to us! If suffering is in the world because human nature is 'fallen', we are all in it together because we are all human. God's purpose for us is something very much better than prosperity or health and strength. Where there is the loss of a loved one, God wants us to see that there is better even than the love of our dear ones. I believe from the bottom of my heart that God's will is that pain and loss and suffering should go, but there is something better even than that. God wants human nature to be remade, to be made good in the best sense of the word, so that it is like Christ's human nature, and I have come to see that suffering is the way by which that can come true. If that is so, then suffering is abundantly

126

worthwhile, and it is a sign, not that God doesn't care, but that he does.

PENTECOST 7

Taking love seriously

> Mark 12.28–31 *They asked him 'Which command-ment is first of all?' Jesus answered, 'The first is, "Hear, O Israel: the Lord our God is the only Lord; love the Lord your God with all your heart, with all your soul, with all your mind, and with all your strength." The second is this: "Love your neighbour as yourself."'*

1 *Trivializing human relationships*

One of the major curses of modern society is trivialization. Marriage is now so trivialized that one in every three marriages in Britain ends in the divorce court. Human dignity is trivialized, when a penny off the income tax is hailed as an increase in living standards. Service is trivialized when a man's labour is measure in terms of 'take-home pay'. And so one could go on with examples from every sphere of modern life.

Behind what is called the permissive society is the trivialization of human relationships. Not long ago an MP sought a debate in the House of Commons, claiming among other things in his motion that 'Divorce is climb-ing even higher; the crime rate among young people is ten times higher than a generation ago; pornography is ram-pant in the service of subversion.' Not surprisingly the debate did not take place, though some of us would be very glad if such vital matters were considered in Parlia-ment.

Meanwhile, despite some excellent programmes, who can seriously deny that the trivialization par excellence is the television medium, daily disgorging its questionable diet to people of all ages? Who can deny that homes are admitting into their lounges material from that source, which even five years ago would have been rejected?

2 *Stable marriage relationships*

What is the Church's answer? Two thousand years ago, St Paul made it quite clear, when he prayed that the love of Christians in Philippi 'may abound yet more and more in knowledge and all discernment; so that you may approve things that are excellent.' He was not advocating knowledge and discernment as a goal in themselves. They were to have a practical result. They were to enable Christians 'to have a sense of what is vital' (to quote a modern Bible version).

Among the things which were vital to St Paul was the sanctity of marriage. Philippi, if not as corrupt as Rome or Corinth, was, nevertheless, a city of moral corruption. Disloyalty, infidelity, promiscuity on the part of husband and wife were common and accepted. It was left to Christians to set an example of family life. It became a vital part of the Christian mission in those days, to establish and maintain sanctified homes and healthy family life. So the Christians in any community stood out against the laxity, perversion and permissiveness, which were the fashion of the times. Who in the Church today can deny that we, as Christians, have this mission placed squarely upon us once more?

Thank God, despite all the pressures from our 'avant garde' mentors, tens of thousands of ordinary men and women find in marriage much happiness, mutual support and contentment. The Prayer Book, which had a knack of hitting the nail on the head, called it an 'honourable estate', and went on to say that it was instituted by God for three purposes. These purposes have in no way been diminished in the Marriage Service as set out in the Alternative Service Book.

The first of these purposes is for the making and bringing up of a family. The second is for the dignifying and beautifying of the sexual relations between one man and one woman. The third is that, as they grow old together, they should be able to support one another. No other life-sharing arrangement has ever been for so long so conspicuously successful. And many young people preparing and being prepared for their marriage still recognize that, in this total commitment to one another, they are safeguarding one of the true marks of stability and sanity in living, which is the Christian's duty throughout these times of moral breakdown.

Appeal

Do not let love of God and love of neighbour get caught up in this modern mood of trivialization. Both are vital for successful living.

PENTECOST 8

The Fruit of the Spirit

Luke 6.35 *'You must love your enemies and do good.'*

Today's Gospel is all about sainthood. Father Andrew once wrote, 'We thank God for all the saints, not only for the canonized ones, but for the saints of God, who in their day and generation responded to the light that they had. We thank God for the Buddha and for the last old woman who died in the workhouse, really believing, really trusting. We think of the great martyrs, of those who by their own lives of holiness have helped others to believe in God and in his goodness.'

1 *Humility*

It has been said by one great student of the spiritual life that there are three characteristic features, which we find in the lives of all the saints—humility, prayer and a life of sacrifice. It would be impossible for the saint to be anything but a humble person. A proud person is that most miserable of all beings, who has never seen anyone greater than himself or herself. The saint lives in the presence of God, in the presence of one supremely greater than himself. This necessarily leads to humility. This is right and natural because true Christian humility means thinking little of oneself and everything of God. Though Uriah Heep in Charles Dickens' *David Copperfield*, professed to be 'a very 'umble man', he was, of course, obsessed by thoughts about himself and his own future, and was anything but humble. Nor is the person, who suffers from what is known as an inferiority complex, necessarily humble. Such persons, who labour under the continuous strain of their own inferiority, may well be self-centered rather than God-centred. In an attempt to restore a sense of their own superiority they may think continually of themselves and seek to draw attention to themselves in every possible way.

The 'difficult' parish worker, who loses no opportunity of making difficulties or raising a voice in protest against this or that, is more often to be pitied than blamed. At the root of it there may be a sense of inferiority, so utterly different from true humility, which it is felt must be overcome by self-assurance. I once heard it said of such a person that 'her great fear in life is that she may not be noticed', but the humility of the saint springs from a sense of nothingness before God. It is the humility which was voiced by the young Isaiah, when he saw the vision of God in the temple, 'Woe is me, for I am a sinful man!' So, too, St Peter, when he saw the glory of Jesus by the lakeside, cried out, 'Depart from me because I am a sinful man, O Lord!' As more and more we see the vision of God, then we become more humble people with a single desire to serve God in all the ways we can. So we should, all of us, priests and people alike, continue to seek the grace of humility, and our blessed Lord is our pattern in humility, as in everything else. The Son of God was a humble man because he never thought of himself for a single moment. 'My meat,' he said, 'is to do the will of him that sent me.' To his disciples he said, 'I am among you as one that serves.' The more we place God first in our lives, the more we become truly humble.

2 *Prayer*

The saints are characterized by their devotion to a life of prayer. There are many definitions of prayer, and one is that prayer is a life lived in the presence of God. We sometimes associate prayer with set times, morning and evening, and with the corporate worship of the Church, but the saints are always conscious of the presence of God, not only when kneeling before the blessed sacrament, but when about their ordinary duties, in office, shop or factory. We need to call to mind frequently, when we are about our ordinary affairs, that we are in the presence of God. What opportunities we all have for cultivating the life of prayer! In many churches in this land the holy sacrifice is offered daily, and the loving invitation of Jesus is given to every one of us to be present and to offer ourselves to the Father, in union with that perfect offering. For many of us progress in the spiritual life may well start with coming during the week on such quiet occasions to offer ourselves more specially to the service of God at the Holy Communion.

3 *Sacrifice*

The saints live lives characterized by sacrifice. It is fatally easy to associate this term, 'sacrifice' only with living a life of poverty or a life free from all human ties. It is true that in their quest for holiness and because of their love of God many of the saints have lived such lives, and do today. In our religious communities we have men and women who, for love of Jesus, have given up all that they have and all hope of home and family; but the spirit of sacrifice ought to characterize the life of every professing Christian. It could be said with truth that we Christian people today show too little sign of being willing to spend and be spent in the Master's service. Coming to an early celebration to receive Holy Communion may mean getting up uncomfortably early; saying prayers morning and evening involves very definite discipline. Giving money one will miss to the work of God's Church means going without things one might like. But the saints of God have always governed themselves by a strong rule embracing these and other things.

'Bearing the cross' is sung about frequently enough, and this means willingness to bear discomfort for the sake of our Lord, and a willingness for the same reason to do without some of those things which the world holds dear, and a readiness to serve our Lord by active work and witness without counting the cost or hoping for a reward.

Conclusion

The study of the lives of the saints is not merely an academic matter for the Christian. We are all 'called to be saints', and to be a saint means to embrace holiness. It may not be attained in its fullness in this present life, but it is, nevertheless, the goal towards which the Christian has to strive. The whole purpose of life is that some day we may see God face to face, and in order to do this the loving help of God is ours today if we will but claim it in God's appointed ways. Draw near to God and he will draw near to you!

PENTECOST 9

A ministry of suffering

Mark 9.22 *'Take pity upon us and help us.'*

1 What causes suffering?

A few weeks ago (Pentecost 6) we thought of Christ healing that blind beggar, Bartimaeus. Here we have a dramatic healing of a boy with convulsions, and we see a loving and lovely father himself agonizing over his boy's illness. Here is an instance of the translation in the New English Bible bringing a family's suffering vividly to life. As we read this striking story of the boy rolling on the ground, foaming at the mouth, well may we ask, 'What is the use of it all?' How many of us have felt like that? There are so many who are bewildered, not least because of the suffering of one very close to them; many who have good cause for being confused by their experiences; one thing after another seems to be arrayed against them, and they say, 'What is the use of trying to go on?' In it all, let us be quite sure of this—God, indeed, wants pain and suffering to go; but surely there is something even better than that. It would not be much use taking away the pain and leaving the cause of it still there. So I believe it is the will of God that the *causes* of suffering should be overcome.

But it is not always easy to see what the causes of suffering are. It is quite certain that we cannot always say that suffering is our own fault; nor can we always blame it on to other people; and we cannot always say that it is due to unfavourable circumstances outside of ourselves, such as bad social conditions. Why do we do these things that bring suffering to others as well as to ourselves? How does it come about that the world, in which we live, is at one and the same time so beautiful, and yet so cruel and so hard? Why is it that a quite normally healthy person finds himself susceptible to all kinds of diseases?

133

I don't think we need to be very clever to see that the real trouble is with human nature itself. There is a fault; there is something inherently wrong with us, and, until we can get back to that and have it corrected and made good, there will always be the possibility of suffering. Yet we are told that we are made in the likeness of God. If that is true, how do we explain this fault in ourselves? We are made in the likeness of God. If we could be again as God made us, we would be free of that fault. Our human nature is 'fallen'; yet we go on living. We still handle the things that God made perfect, though we are imperfect.

Look at it in this way. Imagine a flower garden, and the grass paths among the flowers are soft to tread upon. Into this garden we go with heavy boots on and the spikes cut into the grass as we walk. Suppose our hands are dirty and oily and we take flowers in our hands so that the petals are spoilt. We should feel, perhaps, that we ought to go to the gardener and apologize for the way that we had thoughtlessly spoilt what was beautiful. We might feel that we wanted to do something towards making good what we had spoiled.

Again, have you ever looked into the eyes of a child and thought, 'I wish I had that child's trust and love and simplicity. Yet I am distrustful; my life is never quite free from selfishness. Even when I want to do something that is really good, I cannot be sure that my motive is pure'? Almost we want to go to our heavenly Father and apologize for what we are; and, perhaps, to do something to make reparation for any selfishness that we have introduced into life. But can we make reparation in this way?

Think again of the garden. Suppose we went out of the garden that we had spoiled, made our way home, changed into soft shoes, washed the oil from our hands and came back into the garden: that hasn't made reparation for the spoiling of the garden. Or suppose we say, 'I will not be distrustful any more. I will be unselfish. I will try to do good because it is good.' We still haven't made reparation for the selfishness we brought into life. What we have done is to take steps to prevent ourselves from going on spoiling what is beautiful and good.

3 *A Christian answer*

Now, it is when we apply that to life that the Christian has an answer. The Christian believes two things about Christ. One is that he lived a perfect human life and never caused any suffering; the other is that he himself suffered more than anyone. How are we to explain that?

If we say that suffering really comes from the fact that we are imperfect, how can we account for Christ's sufferings? We say he was perfect, and yet he suffered, and surely that really brings us to the crux of the whole matter. Even if we could suddenly become perfect here and now, that would not undo all the wrong that is in the world. We still would not have made reparation for having spoilt what God made good and beautiful. It would only be if we were to go on suffering that we would begin to make reparation for the past. The Christian can believe that Christ's sufferings are of that sort.

At this point perhaps those of us, who feel that our sufferings are useless and futile, can begin to see where we come in. If Christ lived a real human life, it means that he was really human. If only we can realize this completely, then, without question, it brings fresh hope. We then can think of our sufferings, not as the price that we have to pay for human wickedness, but as something really constructive. Instead of suffering being a bill for damages, it really is a plan for getting things right again, and that is why it is not useless or futile. How can it possibly be useless if it is being used as a way of teaching us humility and patience and love and generosity?

I find that the person, who has really suffered, is almost certain to be more tolerant, because he or she knows then so much that has still to be learnt; and that person has a much deeper love for other people, because personal suffering has taught what selfishness and hatred have done for mankind. This reflection leads on to warmhearted generosity. You even find that people, who have suffered, seem to have a much keener appreciation of what is good and beautiful and are quicker to sense and to resist what is sordid and ugly and selfish. All this must show us something about human nature working towards perfection and experiencing mental or physical suffering.

Nothing good will be lost, but all goodness will be gathered in and made perfect in love. That means that we can begin to see through suffering. Often it appears so overwhelming that it can make us afraid, but there is very definitely a brighter side. It is through suffering that we may be drawn towards God and find our true happiness. Something of the joy, which Christ spoke about, comes to us and it comes to stay.

PENTECOST 10

God is love

> Luke 7.42–3 *Jesus asked, 'Which will love him most?' Simon replied, 'I should think the one that was let off most.' 'You are right', said Jesus.*

1 *A demonstration of love*

In today's moving story of the woman, who had lived an immoral life; who interrupted the party where Jesus was in the Pharisee's house, and poured her treasured possession of oil of myrrh from a small flask over his feet; who was overcome with her tears and her penitence; we have a dramatic illustration of Jesus' scale of values. Sinner that she was, her love placed her high in Jesus' estimation. Later he says, 'Her great love proves that her many sins have been forgiven; where little has been forgiven, little love is shown.' He goes on to forgive her sins.

When you read a story like this, it is almost as though you have climbed many arduous miles in the burning sun and stood now at the mountain top, really seeing the glory that Jesus brought by his words and actions. In a very real sense the whole biblical process lives up to this. We see the writers of the Old Testament groping after love, glimpsing it, missing it, misunderstanding it; but the earlier writers, who saw God as a warlord, gave way to those who portrayed the suffering servant, and they in turn to Jesus and his cross—the unique, unanswerable demonstration of God's love. This, indeed, leads on to the stage, when the writer of the First Letter of St John, 4.16, can say, not that love is *one* of God's characteristics but that 'God is love.'

A sixteen-year old girl came to see me at the Rectory recently and asked, in the way that young people do nowadays, 'Why do you believe in God?' I didn't know her—she was at a local sixth-form college—but I was delighted to tell her that I didn't start with such a belief: I finished there. She asked me where I *had* started, and I said 'With Jesus. I admired him and I thought he was right. I think the things he stood for were right. He showed a way of love, which is the most important thing that there is for me.' My young friend went on, 'This doesn't tell me why you believe in God.' My answer was, 'It is because I believe in these things about Jesus, that they matter more than anything else; that then I have to believe in a God of love. But I don't start there; I finish there.' Her reply was, 'I can't believe much about Christianity, but I do believe in love.'

2 *The worth of love*

Now, that girl is not untypical of her generation; many of them believe in love; of course, it is sometimes sentimental, sometimes sexual, and there may have been an element of these things in the woman portrayed in today's Gospel; but this is not always the case. Many today amongst our young people protest about colour; they raise money for Oxfam and Shelter and Christian Aid. It may fall short of the full understanding of Christian love, but we do well to remember that our Lord said of this woman today, 'Her great love proves that her many sins have been forgiven.'

137

He also said to the young lawyer, who came to see that love of God and man were more important than religious observances, 'You are not far from the kingdom of God.' 'God is love', said the writer of the First Letter of John. What does that mean?

It affirms the worth and reality of every form of love. Most people know that modern translations of the Bible usually give 'love' for three different Greek words. One is primarily concerned with sexuality—*eros*, represented by the little statue in Piccadilly; one primarily with friendship—*philia*; and one with Christian self-giving without expectation of return—*agape*. It is the last which is used exclusively in the New Testament, and particularly in the famous 1 Corinthians 13 poem on love. In fact, it is not, I think, possible always to distinguish between the three, and we ought not to try. To do this, in my view, can be biblically ill-based, theologically disastrous, psychologically absurd and practically impossible, for friendship can have within it a sexual element, which gives it warmth and depth, though it may never lead to sexual intercourse. Friendship can lead to self-giving, just as the force of water can be used for the welfare of mankind. So can the force of sex be harnessed to meet and to serve human need. So one could go on! Because we are persons, the various kinds of love interact within us. All human love, which expresses itself in concern, in compassion, in affection or in trust, is valuable and good, and, if we are honest, does anything matter quite so much as to be loved and to be allowed to love?

3 *The infinity of love*

To say, 'God is love' is to affirm the worth and reality of the whole of human love. But, of course, it is to affirm more, if it is to affirm, not only the reality but the infinity of love. Human love is very wonderful, but it is also very fickle, very disappointing, and even sometimes very cruel. The failure of human love can lead you to disbelieve in love altogether, but it can drive you to the love of God. To say, therefore, that God is love is to turn to a new dimension. To be a Christian is to take a bet in the infinite and eternal love of God, to stake one's life on this one certainty, in a world otherwise full of change and decay.

PENTECOST 11

Freedom and authority

> Matthew 20.16 '*Thus will the last be first, and the first last.*'

The amount of free choice in life may be sometimes rather terrifying. Whilst there are many who profess that they like things this way, there are others who are constantly seeking more direction. The truth is that life at its best is a combination of God's general direction of laws being freely used by us to live in his Spirit. Today's parable reminds us that his assessment of our importance is different from ours. Whether we are called at the third, sixth, ninth or eleventh hour, we are nevertheless called upon to work for the kingdom. There is no preferential treatment.

1 *Distinctiveness and obedience*

There are then two divisions which jostle one another in the Christian's heart—the instinct for separateness and the instinct to be obedient to some authority. It is easy to follow the first and much more difficult to follow the second. Yet we never become integrated unless we acknowledge both these instincts and provide for them both to be satisfied.

The Gospel of Jesus Christ provides for both. Our distinctiveness has been fully acknowledged by God. 'You are of more value than many sparrows,' he says. What we find so difficult to understand is that only by being obedient children of God do we make real the uniqueness of our distinctiveness. In short, we will never feel how important we really are unless we are obedient to God. We must be a people living under authority.

2 The need for authority

In the ordinary everyday affairs of living we fully acknowledge the necessity of authority. Man can only exist as part of an order when he is a member of a community. And if living under authority is of the essence of a civilized existence, is it not also true that the existence of the Church in the world as an effective, comforting power depends upon whether her children are obedient or disobedient to her laws? The Church has no policemen to impose the laws it makes, of course. Her weapons are the pulpit, the printed word and the sacraments.

Not long ago I had a letter asking for more guidance and leadership from the pulpit, and I have dealt with much of what that gentleman said in another sermon. He uttered a good deal of truth, but there is certainly this to be said on the other side. We may try to give a lead, but the effect of what we say depends upon what is going on in the listener's heart. Nothing can result from our preaching unless the hearer is willing to admit the authority of the Church as a governing influence in life. Unless this is admitted, preaching is futile.

People say, 'Is it not true that religion is purely an individual matter? An active membership in the life of the Church is no more incumbent upon us than a share in the music society and carrying less obligation?' How many indeed expect to worship as they please and to transfer their allegiance from one body to another with as little notice of any obligation as if we were changing the dentist? Rules, too, when announced in the pulpit, are often resented. Any attempt to declare that Church membership excludes some things and obliges us to perform others is seen as a direct interference with our right to investigate and to choose. Attempts to advise certain forms of self-discipline and worship are often pushed aside as narrow and sectarian.

3 *Authority and freedom in the Church of England*

The Church of England is the most comprehensive and tolerant Church in Christendom, but it has its authority and its means of voicing this authority. The authority is represented in the Scriptures, the creeds, the worship and the resolutions of the Bishops in Convocation. A man must be free to accept or reject Christ as Lord. A man must be free to examine the teaching of the various Churches, so as to determine which stands nearest to the ideal of our Lord; but once he has accepted his Lordship in the Church, which he finds nearest to his Master, then I believe the society of believers, which we call the Church, claims his loyalty and his obedience.

I am not ashamed to confess that I often thank God that I am a member of the Church of England. I believe that I belong to a Church rich in the thoughts and the instincts, the conflicts and the hopes, the sorrows and the love, the joy and the splendour of all our fellow Christians who have gone before. Their prayers, their wisdom, their loyalty lives on in the worship and the hallowed traditions of so many of our ancient parish churches. Here is gathered all that is abiding in character, the beauty of holiness, the strength of self-mastery, the agelong tenderness of humanity mingled with tears of penitence, the pity and piety of little things, and the gracious remembrance of the saints.

For year after year her public prayers have been offered, her round of fast and festival, her ordered activity, her sacraments of grace, her faithful preaching of the Word of God. If we are wise, we think more of the Christian family and less of ours; more of her claims and less of our rights—very much more; but, at all times, of the strange providence which has called us to be saints in the Church of England.

141

PENTECOST 12

The witness in community

Matthew 5.14 *'You are light for all the world.'*

In the large parish, of which I am privileged to be the Rector, I recently reflected with members of my staff on the thousand or so candidates that we had presented for Confirmation in the preceding ten years. We were concerned at those who had become indifferent in their Christian life, and we reflected what a transformation there would have been, had all of them carried forward the glimpse they had had of Christian discipleship, which they appeared to see with such clarity at the time that they knelt before the Bishop.

1 *Commitment*

Whether Confirmation takes place in adolescence or adult life, it is always true to speak of it as our biggest self-commitment. We carefully examine a definite way of life, which, if we take it seriously, is certain to affect every department of it, and, when we have made this examination, we solemnly pledge ourselves to the acceptance of the Christian religion, as it is practised in the Church of England. We make its creeds and its sacraments our own, and we enter into full membership of the greatest society in the world, the Holy Catholic Church. From now onwards, we may well believe, our churchmanship is going to be the background to our family and business life. It will colour all our varied relationships and will largely govern our thoughts on the great problems of life and love and marriage and parenthood and death and the hereafter.

2 *Unfulfilled commitment*

Unhappily, a large percentage of those who are confirmed, year by year, have not really troubled to face up to what is

142

involved in these new responsibilities, with the result that, between their outward profession of faith and the actual expression of it in life and in conduct, there has been a tragic gap. Many respectable communicants would probably be shocked if they were told that their Christianity did not resemble the religion of its founder, but we have to face the fact that this remains true, and it is a big stumbling-block in the spread of the Church's evangelistic work.

There is a prayer, of which frequent use is made today. It is a fine one, but the honest praying of it requires courage and humility: 'Teach us, good Lord, to serve thee as thou deservest; to give and not to count the cost; to fight and not to heed the wounds; to toil and not to seek for rest; to labour and not to ask for any reward, save that of knowing we do thy will; through Jesus Christ, our Lord.'

We measure our religion against that prayer. Where are we now?—not very far, because we make a habit of doing just those things which this prayer tries to help us combat. Now the undertakings we make at our Confirmation are nothing less than revolutionary, because they are the direct opposite of the way of the world and its superficially attractive scale of values. As members of the Body of Christ we are called to a service which is its own reward, and it cannot be done without the secret behind such lives, and that is a personal relationship to a loving and everpresent Christ. That is the first and last condition of true churchmanship, a personal loyalty to a living person, Jesus of Nazareth, the image of the invisible God.

3 Commitment expressed

(a) At the altar

Along with this realization of a supreme divine friendship comes the great desire to express it in practical terms, and there is no avenue of expression which can compare with that of communicant membership. Our first and most obvious duty and privilege is frequent approach to the altar, where we kneel, as Evelyn Underhill so perfectly describes it, 'on the frontiers of the unseen world'. It is here that we give and receive; we love and are loved; we speak and are spoken to. It is for this reason that the central place of the Lord's own service is desirable for each church worshipper. It is the only thing that brings our Christian fellowship into a really worshipping one, and it is a high but attainable ideal that all Church members should aim at, to be present at the celebration of Holy Communion on every Sunday and holy day. To the committed Christian, far from asking a great deal, it is little enough if our religion is to us the most important thing in the world.

What, after all, is the Church of God and what is its purpose in the world? It is the great society of the baptised, the living and the dead, brought into being by Jesus Christ, a society through which the Holy Spirit moves and works. St Paul calls the Church the Body of Christ, meaning that, as at Bethlehem, the second person of the Trinity took to himself a human body, by means of which to present himself to men; so Christ reveals himself to the world today through that body of people which we call the Church— which is, solemn thought, you and me! By our Baptism we are made members of Christ's Body, the Church; and within that Body we may, if we will, be fed with the grace of God.

It is our duty, as members of Christ's Church, to be present at its meetings in Church and, in particular, at the Lord's own service. Historically, Matins came into existence as a service of preparation for the Holy Communion, and Evensong as a thanksgiving for it. As my old college tutor used to say, 'The Holy Communion is the jewel in the setting of Matins and Evensong, for it is at the Holy Communion that we obey our Lord's dying command, "Do this in remembrance of me."' It is there that we realize more than anywhere our membership of the family of God, and it is hard to understand how any thinking Christian can fail to be present regularly at the service which Christ himself gave us.

The Church was intended by our Lord to be a family of people united to him in the power of the Holy Spirit, in the bond of an unswerving love and obedience. The instructed

Christian attends church to worship—to give God his worth—and not necessarily to be edified or amused; nor do we attend church that we may feel better for going. We approach God in worship, not so much for what we may obtain, but that we may give him 'our bounden duty and service'.

(b) In the world

It is only when this side of our life has been put right, and when our duty of worship is being done well, that we shall be able to carry out the work of the Church amongst those outside the Church, who so greatly need the Church's message of hope. We are to be shepherds, caring for our flocks, and also fishermen casting our nets into the larger waters of the world, in order to land men and women on to the rock, which is Christ. That twofold calling belongs not only to priests but to the whole Church. We are members of the one organization (as Archbishop William Temple used to say), which exists not for its own members primarily, but for outsiders. We are expected to love and to pray and to work for the extension of Christ's kingdom, by witness amongst all with whom we come into contact. If you are going to leave this great work to the desperately understaffed ranks of the clergy, then the Church will become stagnant and lost in parochial matters, and its true glory will never even be glimpsed in the world outside.

An appeal

This is the life of the communicant member, who takes his life seriously—regular worship, public and private, and the practical expression of that worship in the generous giving of time, talents and money for the work of Christ at home and abroad, and the conduct of every department of life, as is befitting to one who owes his first allegiance to Jesus Christ. More than anything else is the Church of England in need of men and women of this calibre; those who have glimpsed the vision and have steadfastly refused to ignore it; those who have knelt at the foot of the cross and have received shelter; those who have met a guide on the highway of life and have cast away their own uncertain charts for ever. Ours is a great and high calling, and our Lord's words are addressed to us, 'You are light for all the world. When a lamp is lit, it is put on a lamp-stand, where it gives light to everyone.'

PENTECOST 13

Peacemakers

> Matthew 10.16 *'I send you out like sheep among wolves.'*

The pulpit is not a place, in which to produce solutions to the bloodshed still going on all around us or that which threatens to engulf us. Our world is too complex. But what we have to do from time to time in a Christian service is to ask what is the nature of Christian peace? The nature of the peace extolled, for example, in the beatitudes: Blessed are the peace*makers*. What does it mean to be peace*makers*?

1 *False peacemaking*

It is clear in the Bible that there is a false peace as well as a true peace. Prophets in the Old Testament were condemned for crying, 'Peace, peace!', when there was no peace. In this same Gospel of St Matthew Jesus spoke of coming to bring 'not peace, but a sword', and certainly the kingdom of God will always mean controversy and will always bring division—because it demands decisions from individuals and from societies. There certainly is a kind of peace which contracts out of the world's problems, and it is indifferent to its sorrows. It has been described as being 'like the peace of a stagnant pond, with a green scum of selfishness on top'.

Some of the early fathers of the Church interpreted our Lord's call to be peace*makers* only in a spiritual sense, and

146

saw it as applauding those who appropriate the peace of God for themselves. Now it is true that the Gospel is about reconciliation with God and that only from that are we able to offer reconciliation with one another. But the background of the Gospel is Jewish, and high on the list of Hebrew priorities was that of just relationships.

2 True peacemaking

To be reconciled to God is to be the agent of reconciliation in his world. Since we inherit that tradition there can be no distinction between what is called the evangelical gospel and what is called the social gospel. The two belong together; to love God is to love our neighbour. The lovely Jewish greeting, Shalom, means that you wish another person all that makes for his or her good. So, then, peace is a strong word. It means very much more than the absence of war. It means the establishment of a just society and it means compassionate relationships within it. Our Lord's blessing in the beatitudes rests upon the peace*makers* and not on peace-*lovers*. It is not difficult to be a *lover* of peace in today's violent and divided and disordered and unjust world. Indeed, you would have to be pretty blinkered if you were not. But it is quite exceptionally hard to be a peace*maker*, because one is always being accused then of compromising, when one seeks a solution of difficulties. You will always be attacked by extremists and militants of either side, and this will be compounded with suggestions of justice and right, and all kinds of emotive expressions are brought into play. As all, who try to be leaders in local government and beyond, know only too well, it is far easier to attack solutions than to defend them—and that is as true of Church history as of the secular.

3 The call to peacemaking

Each one of us is called to be a peace*maker*, and, because we spend most of our lives in our own parishes and districts, we had better start there if we are called to be peace*makers*, in whatever sphere that we find ourselves.

But if we have this deep conviction about real justice and real compassion, then we should always also be on the lookout for other spheres in which to find ourselves, because the peace*maker* can never be unmoved by war and its consequent suffering and obscenity. Jesus is called a peace*maker*, the Son of God, because he shares the mind and will of the Father, which is that men and women should be reconciled to him and so to one another.

One of those, who suffered and died in the second world war, was Dietrich Bonhoeffer, who still haunts this generation. In his book, *The Cost of Discipleship*, he wrote: 'The followers of Jesus have been called to peace, but now they are told—they must not only have peace, but make it. His disciples keep the peace by choosing to endure suffering and humiliation, rather than inflict it upon others. They maintain fellowship where others would break it off. The peace*makers* carry the cross with their Lord, for it was on the cross that the real peace was made.'

PENTECOST 14

What to pray for

Luke 11.9 *'Ask, and you will receive.'*

1 *Asking for things*

That being so, it is not merely childish to ask God for things. Asking for things is not a kind of prayer that mature Christians should have outgrown. There are plenty of people, who say that it is all very well for children to ask God for this and that when they say their prayers, but that, when we grow up, we should put away such childish ideas and give up the practice of writing God begging letters. This notion that asking prayers are wrong or somewhat improper is quite mistaken. There is a rather similar cliché that 'we ought to come to church, not to get but to give.' It is doubtful, however, whether many of us have much to give to God.

In the Bible the typical form of prayer is making requests to God and thanking him if they are granted; and if they are not granted, then still praising the Father's name and bowing the head. There are kinds of mysticism, which teach that the higher sort of prayer transcends asking God for things and simply becoming absorbed in contemplation. I suggest that that is not for the general congregation, and perhaps not for you and me.

2 *Priorities in asking*

As long as we are in this world we shall never get beyond asking God for things. In the Book of Common Prayer (which I hope you still turn to sometimes) there is a prayer for 'all sorts and conditions of men', and we may also pray for all sorts and conditions of things. All the same, there is much room for discrimination. In particular, there is the question of what should occupy the first place in our prayers, what the second place, and so on. The Lord's Prayer is the best standard by which to check our own prayers. All the way through the Lord's Prayer we ask God for things of one kind or another. But see what comes first.

(a) For God's will to be done
'Hallowed by thy name, Thy kingdom come, Thy will be done, on earth as it is in heaven.' So, if we love God above all things, we shall pray first of all for the things *he* wants. We shall pray that his name may be hallowed by a recovery of reverence; reverence for the mysterious being of God himself, reverence for nature, which is his creation, reverence for every man since every man is made in the image of God, however much the image may have been defaced. We shall pray that God's kingdom may come on earth—by the deliverance of mankind from fear, by the establishment of justice and peace among the nations, by

the rekindling of a passion for truth, and by the opening of springs of mercy and compassion. We shall pray that God's will may be done on earth—in what we ourselves do and say and think, in the fulfilment of the work we do with others in the relationships of ordinary life. If we are going to hunger and thirst after righteousness, it is things like that we shall pray for first.

(b) For material things for ourselves
But the Lord's Prayer does not stop there. It goes on, 'Give us this day our daily bread.' So, our prayers do not always have to be for spiritual things. We may rightly pray for material things like bread and the means of physical subsistence. We know now that there is no sharp cleavage between material and spiritual things or between mind and body. They are intimately connected and dependent upon one another.

When I was first ordained, my one and only vicar, who looked after me for the three years before I was a priest-in-charge and had to make the decisions myself, said to me, 'It is not much good talking to these people about crowns in heaven, when what many of them need is half-a-crown on earth.' That is a parable that could be applied to many things. It is true that Holy Scripture lays it down that 'man does not live by bread alone'; but the Lord recognizes that we do all need bread and what bread stands for, in order to live a tolerable human life, and we are quite right to bring this into our prayers.

(c) For material things for others
Notice that we are taught to pray not 'give me my daily bread,' but 'give us our daily bread.' We pray to the Father of all for the whole human family. That is why, if we are going to be literal-minded, it makes good sense for us last thing at night, to pray, 'give us this day our daily bread,' for when we are going to bed a new day is beginning in other parts of the world, and when we say the Lord's Prayer we are praying for them as well as for ourselves.

Of course, we could not pray with integrity that all our

fellow human beings may have their daily bread, if we were not prepared to do everything in our power to see that they *do* have it. Happily, in this country, despite an amazing amount of discontent, there is very little need for any to be below the breadline. But it ought to be a very disturbing thought indeed to us Christians in Europe and America that, while all the time we are trying to maintain and, indeed, to raise our material standard of living, there are many millions of people in the East, who certainly have not the bare necessities of life. There is still far too little desire amongst many people in this land to support any measures calculated to improve their condition, and this is because of such people's concern that our own way of life might suffer somewhat in consequence. So it is a good thing when our prayers do disturb our consciences about matters like this.

(d) For forgiveness
Then, 'Forgive us . . . as we forgive.' Forgiveness, too, is a universal and basic human need. It is a melancholy fact that there are multitudes of human beings well-fed, more or less in the lap of luxury, but at the same time wretched and miserable because their human relationships are wrong and poisoned. It may be their relationship with their own family or with their neighbours; or with their fellow-workers and with their colleagues or some public body on which they serve; or with the members of some society, to which they belong; very likely a society which is supposed to be doing excellent work. There are many societies and individuals, whose good work is spoilt, because the human relationships of those engaged in it are poisoned by jealousy, or resentment, or secret grudges, or unhealed quarrels.

Only forgiveness can cure these diseases, the forgiveness of God flowing out into the forgiveness of one another. This is certainly a thing for which we ought to pray. If, instead of nursing grievances, people would speak of them openly to God and ask that he would impart to us all the spirit of forgiveness and reconciliation, and the courage, if need be, to take the first step towards putting matters right, our human existence would be a great deal happier and a little less unlike what God intends it to be.

(e) For deliverance from evil

Finally, 'Lead us not into temptation, but deliver us from evil.' Temptation here means the trials that compass our life on earth—they are always round the corner, even if they are not in the actual path we are treading. To ask not to be led into temptation is to acknowledge that we are easily put out by it, and that we easily succumb, and that we are not very good at taking it. It is a confession that we have no ground on which to be bubbling over with self-confidence.

The Lord's Prayer shows that we may rightly ask to be spared those temptation and ordeals, which often in the past have discovered the weakness of our defences. At the same time it recognizes that we live in a world where much must be that offends God, so we are told to pray also, 'Deliver us from evil.' God alone can preserve us in the trials and perils, through which we must pass. He rules the raging of the sea, and when the waves arise he can still them.

Conclusion

So let us learn how to pray and for what to pray. Material things for ourselves and for others? Yes, but firstly for what God wants of us and for forgiveness and for his protection. As the Book of Common Prayer so often reminds us, God has promised to answer our prayers. Our Lord said, 'Ask and you will receive.'

PENTECOST 15

Young people

Matthew 14.7 *He took an oath to give her anything she cared to ask.*

Today's Gospel is a remarkable story of one in authority pandering to the misguided whim of a child. John the Baptist was killed because he showed up the sin of Herodias, who had left Philip, her husband, for his brother, Herod. First she had John imprisoned, and later arranged for her teenage daughter to dance before the lascivious and half-mad Herod, prior to asking for John's head on a dish.

1 *What the young have*

Well may one wonder what the effect of such a boon granted would be on the child! I hope it won't be thought too wire-drawn if I draw from this stark Gospel a few thoughts about relationships between adults and children. Let me read you a quote: 'The world is passing through troubled times. The young people of today think of nothing but themselves. They have no reverence for parents or old age. They are impatient of all restriction. They talk as if they alone know everything, and what passes for wisdom with us is foolishness with them. As for the girls, they are immodest and unwomanly in speech, behaviour and dress.'

Now that is not a newspaper article describing the young people of the twentieth century; it is an extract from the writings of Peter the Hermit in 1272. It is a timely reminder of the need for balanced perspectives when we think about young people. It is so easy to be negative, but it is a fact that some of the greatest achievements in history have been accomplished by teenagers. Schubert composed his D Major Symphony at the age of sixteen. As we have seen through talented musicians locally, if we will only

153

encourage and help, young people are capable of rising to great heights in music, and it is abundantly true in other areas also. But it is easy to be negative. You could, for example, make out a very good case for bringing Romeo and Juliet before a juvenile court, as minors in need of care and protection.

2 *What the young need*

So how can we help young people to channel their energy and idealism positively? Surely only by increasing our understanding and considering their basic needs. An adult has been defined as a person who has stopped growing at both ends and begun to grow in the middle. It is, perhaps, fair to say that adolescents are those who are still growing at both ends, and the two ends have not yet become fused at the middle. Maybe the basic needs of young people can be summarized as follows:

(a) The need to adjust to physical changes. The young person realizes the awful responsibility of being free to be irresponsible and the magnitude of the fact that at last he or she is becoming a person with individuality.

(b) The need to adjust their ambitions to their real capacity. Most young people have high-minded ideas about what they wish to do with their lives. Often help is needed to discover the actual, rather than the imagined, potential and their own individual talents and abilities.

(c) The need to adjust to the imperfections of human relationships. Young people struggle to free themselves from parental guidance and authority; yet, paradoxically, they feel great need for an adult listening-post. They copy adult behaviour; yet they are often puzzled by adult conduct, which can be as irrational as their own.

(d) The need to learn a communal code. All young people need some family to belong to and to experience belonging. Often the jump from a family-centred and school-centred life into the adult world can be a frightening one. The need is to see that a community life is dependent upon the individual contribution.

(e) The need to become an individual. Adolescence is marked, above all, by the question, 'Who am I?' The process of self-discovery can often be a traumatic one for the individual as well as his family.

(f) The need of a faith to live by. This period is marked by the search for purpose and meaning in life. All the signs are that the younger generation today are undertaking this search with more eagerness and idealism than ever before.

This catalogue does not, I hope, sound pretentious or condescending; it is intended to be accurate. To any young person hearing these words, I say, by all means make out your own list of the needs of the older generation! It would be an illuminating exercise, and might even lead to greater mutual understanding.

3 *What the Church should offer*

But what of the Church in this situation? The aim of the Church of Christ in the world is to build up the people of God, so our aim for young people is not less than this—to build up the younger part of God's community in the loving fellowship of Christ's Church. This is a demanding programme, calling for sympathy, compassion, skill and great patience. It demands that all the older members of the Church community understand, accept and approve of this aim, and are prepared to make certain sacrifices of one sort or another, to see this aim effectively achieved. It also means that, if we wish young people to play their proper part in the life of our Church family, we must be prepared to be challenged, to see that the life, which we profess, is realized in fact. They wish to *see* love by community members.

Again, if we wish to help young people in their search for meaning, we must be prepared to listen. We must be prepared to take their suggestions seriously. There must be give and take. It is possible for a seventeen-year-old to be a member of the Parochial Church Council. Many might feel that a generous representation of this age group in each church council would be a distinct advantage.

155

The Church *can* satisfy the deepest needs of our young people today. Many people profess an anxiety about our young; but are we Christians prepared to act out of our anxiety? However unfairly (and is it really unfair?) the Church of Christ will be judged by young people, not on her ideals or her faith, but on the way that her members live. And it boils down to this—do we care enough?

PENTECOST 16

A sufficient revelation

> Luke 16.19–20 *'There was once a rich man, who dressed in purple and the finest linen, and feasted in great magnificence every day. At his gate, covered with sores, lay a poor man named Lazarus, who would have been glad to satisfy his hunger with the scraps from the rich man's table.'*

This parable may be regarded as a drama divided into three scenes. Its keynote is the contrast between two lives, and in each scene the contrast is strikingly preserved.

Scene 1

In the first scene two men are living in the world. One the world has smiled on. He is rich, popular, one of the world's great men; and a religious man, too, as his address to 'Father Abraham' shows. He lived as rich men live, well-dressed and eating sumptuously; in other words, he lived according to his station; and nothing very wrong in that, you may say. At his door was a beggar, Lazarus, and there was nothing uncommon for such a one to be neglected. He was in extreme need and very ill—perhaps, as he gazed on the rich man's plenty, thinking of that strange problem, God's providence. His name, Lazarus, means, 'God is my Saviour', showing that he, too, in the story had trust in God; and sorely was he tried.

Scene 2

In the second scene we are shown something that is the one certain factor in all our lives—the death of them both. The rich man's death with every comfort, followed by a grand funeral with crowds of friends, the hired mourners, the procession through the streets, the burning of spices, the grand tomb, the funeral oration and then the epitaph relating the achievements of the deceased, no doubt including the building of a synagogue. On the other deathbed, everything mean and poor, just what the law required. If this were all the drama, the drama would be tame, for it is all common enough.

Scene 3

But our Lord lifts the curtain and then, in the great unseen world, the contrast continues. The rich man is said to be tormented, not by the arbitrary judgment of God, but by the working out of the unchangeable law of his own life. Now he realizes the responsibility of life and what a solemn thing it is. He has indeed now torment of sight, of taste and of memory—torment of sight because he had formerly feasted his eyes on art and beauty, torment of taste for he now longed for a drop of water, and torment of memory, which was probably the worst of all. 'Son, remember,' says Abraham, and he does so only too well with all the sins of his past life and its consequences brought before him. 'It was my own fault; I had a daily call and paid no attention,' he could well say.

The rich man is human and begins to make excuses. The request is made to send Lazarus to his family to warn them; and this is an accusation against God that he was unjust in not giving him sufficient warning. It is probable that his motive was a desire to justify himself and suggesting that God did not give a strong enough warning to compel obedience. The reply comes that his family has Moses and the prophets to guide them. What could be plainer than God's accredited revelation? The rich man

157

was probably a Pharisee, who would have known what Isaiah had said about hell, but he did not act on what he professed to believe. He argues that a special supernatural manifestation would convince his family and would have saved him. He is told that those, who will not act on the accredited revelation of God, will not act on special supernatural manifestations. The Jews indeed were later tested in this. One *did* rise from the dead—our Lord himself. They tried by fraud to conceal the fact of his resurrection; they were not challenged and comforted by it.

The lesson of the drama

This story is always with us. Men complain of God that his revelation is not sufficiently full to compel obedience. That is usually an excuse to justify neglect or violation of what has been revealed. Sufficient has been revealed to guide millions through this world. We have as much as all the saints have had. We profess often to believe it, and it is our fault if we do not act on what we say we believe. Those who do not use the light they have, and which they recognize, would not use more if it were given to them.

If we had miracles and supernatural phenomena we would explain them away as a result of imagination. Therefore, God has given enough for the faculty of faith to grasp. Miracles generally do not help faith, and without faith no amount of evidence produces moral conviction. This is shown by the fact that those, who ask for convincing evidence of the truth of Christianity, are those who reject or explain away the miraculous part of the evidence which they have. In this story our Lord is prophesying that his resurrection will not convert those, whom his teaching has not touched. Only to those, who act on the light that they have, is more given.

PENTECOST 17

False faith and true faith

> Luke 7.9 'I tell you, nowhere, even in Israel, have I found faith like this.'

My subject is: false faith and true faith.

1 Two errors

It seems to me that there are two recurring themes in false faiths. Firstly that a particular person has some sort of mystical experience, whereby he may feel convinced that the rest of Christendom has gone astray and that he is divinely commanded to put things right. On finding that little impression is made on the Christian Church, a new society is formed with the same monotonous battle-cry, 'Salvation is with us; the rest are wrong!' We then are at the position where a multitude of clamorous voices are heard, proclaiming that they are right; and it is completely understandable that the person in the pew may well ask, 'Who is right and where is the truth to be found?'

Secondly, each of these sects claims that what they believe and practise is supported by infallible scriptural evidence. With remarkable diligence and method a battery of random texts, invariably out of context, is produced to prove their points. The question must, therefore, be asked, 'Did God intend us to be left perplexed as to what we ought to believe about himself and his dealings with us?' Is it not more consistent with all his dealings with us, that he would provide for us the means whereby we may come to know the truth, that there should be one flock and one shepherd?

2 The Church and the Bible

It is from this turmoil of contradiction that we turn to the catholic doctrine of the Church and the Bible. It has to be

159

said that, in doing so, we part company with any who would deny us the use of our faculty of God-given reasoning, whereby we must bring to our study the findings of science, philosophy and historical criticism, which things are forbidden by the sects to which I refer.

When we quote from Holy Scripture it must be in context and in the framework of all the knowledge that we have about the points under discussion. In scrutinizing our beliefs we must, therefore, appeal to the whole primitive tradition of the early Church, not only the Scriptures but the sacraments, the creeds and the historical episcopate, that entire framework which surrounded the life and death of Christ, and the apostles who followed him.

The results of such an investigation expose immediately the greatest of all sectarian errors, namely that they fail to see that the Church preceded the Scriptures in time. In the first three hundred years of the Church's existence there was no Bible as we know it today. The authority in matters of faith and morals was centred in the apostles and their apostolic descendants gathered in council, and not in an 'infallible book'. They alone held the authority of deciding what was God's word and what was not. As they did that, they gave us the Canon of Holy Scripture, selecting the books to be the present Bible from many others of a disputed nature.

Whether they like it or not, our sectarian friends have derived their 'infallible book' from the Church, whose jurisdiction they now reject. Jesus did not give his disciples a copy of the Bible and say, 'In this alone you will find the truth about God!' Rather the burden of those three epoch-making years was to train twelve men to think clearly about himself and prepare them to assume positions of authority in the Church, which he was to bring into being at Pentecost. The Church of England stands in direct line of succession from these early apostles, embodying within herself this same divine authority given to the first apostles by our Lord.

Notwithstanding, the catholic Church holds Holy Scripture in great veneration, believing that these Scrip-

160

tures are the embodiment of the early tradition and, as such, must be used to prove all that she teaches. At the same time she holds with equal veneration her responsibility as keeper of these Scriptures, and reserves the right to interpret and explain them by the aid of the Holy Spirit of truth given to her by her Lord. The historic episcopate, gathered in council, is the body who may interpret what the Bible says in matters of faith and morals—cut yourself off from its life and you have sectarianism with its 'confusion worse confounded'.

Conclusion

So, any person, be it Charles Russell, Mary Eddy, John Thomas or Mr Moon, who claims that God has sent them with a new message, must have his or her claims tested against the Scriptures as interpreted by the apostolic Church. God would not have in one instant established a means whereby the truth is to be known, and then at other times have sent along other individuals, each with their own interpretation of the facts, to create new bodies, in some cases hardly meriting the name of Christian.

Every man may question what he believes; but let the catholic Christian do so in all humility with an instructed conscience, remembering that no attack against the Church is ever an entirely new one. All of these heresies have appeared in one form or another in the Church's life in its past. While men remain sinful characters they will, no doubt, go on appearing. But the ancient Church still stands and will do so, unmoved by the petty heretical ideas of man; and it will stand until its founder and builder returns, because he himself once said, 'I will build my Church, and the gates of hell shall not prevail against it.'

PENTECOST 18

Responsibility

> Matthew 25.21 *'Well done, my good and trusty servant! You have proved trustworthy in a small way; I will now put you in charge of something big.'*

1 *Responsibility in acceptance of duty*

'What an irresponsible person you are!' We have all heard that remark made, sometimes with justification, when we have let someone down. Perhaps we have sometimes pitied people rather patronizingly, as not being responsible for their actions. What is this responsibility which we expect and require of ourselves and of others? Responsibility means that we can be trusted, that we can be counted upon to do what we undertake and what is expected of us; that we can take the initiative and do things without having to be told. It is the acceptance of duty rather than the perennial shout for rises and privileges; it means that we have reached the years of discretion. We can plan and carry out actions; we can make decisions and give an account for them.

2 *The Church's responsibility*

One of the gravest problems of the day is the evasion of their responsibilities by vast numbers of people in all walks of life. It affects every calling. The clergy must be the first to admit many failures in the exercise of our great responsibility. What a different place the world would be if each of us even tried to know and to do what we ought to do! Now the Church has a duty to put, first before her members and then to all others who will listen, the statement of the twofold duty required of all—duty to God and duty to neighbour. The exposition of these twin duties or responsibilities is a major part of the Church's teaching. For the carrying out of the worship of God and the service of our

162

fellow men God has liberally endowed each of us with precisely the talents (or, as we would say, the abilities and skills), and also with the possessions, that we need to enable us to fulfil our responsibilities. These things are not ours. We have nothing and we are nothing. They are lent to us by God to use in his service, and we shall be answerable to him when we die for that use, misuse or failure to use them; all of which is so dramatically shown in the Gospel for today.

3 The responsibility of giving

In addition to this proper use of possessions, time and ability, man has always made a direct offering to God of a representative proportion of these things, so that the whole may be sanctified. That is true from when Cain and Abel in Genesis brought their offering of the first fruits and the firstling of the flocks. This has been continued all down the ages, not only to Harvest Thanksgiving offerings, but in our alms and gifts that we present over and above the payment of our dues—a small return to God for the many blessings that he has given us.

Now a great deal of irresponsibility in the fulfilment of our duty to God has crept in during past years. The generosity to God and his Church in former years dwindled and was left to the few faithful. This loss of responsibility resulted in totally inadequate finance for the maintenance, let alone the expansion, of the Church. Vital repairs to the fabric were neglected; church workers were grossly ill-paid; recruits to the ministry dried up; missionary work was not supported. In an attempt to remedy this situation all sorts and methods of raising finance were resorted to—bazaars, jumble sales, whist drives, football pools and, occasionally, the big appeal and subscription list.

4 Christian stewardship

In more recent years there has arisen a new spirit, which is totally dissatisfied with that situation and has sought to remedy it. It has almost exactly coincided with the years that I have been an incumbent. Just as there have been evangelistic missions to awaken Christians to their spiritual responsibilities, so a great mission wave, called Christian stewardship, is taking hold of the Church throughout the world to call men and women to their great responsibilities in putting the Church's house in order. No longer are Christian people asking, 'What does the Church want or need?', but, 'What ought I to give to God? My sense of responsibility is shown by the response I make.

PENTECOST 19

Self-reproach

Luke 19.8 'He has gone in,' they said, 'to be the guest of a sinner.'

Whenever I read this story of Jesus seeing this little man, Zacchaeus, hiding in a tree and putting him so squarely in the middle of the picture, I find myself moved by the picture of self-reproach and remorse presented by this man to us. Jesus explains it all and transforms it. We all know only too well how worry and anxiety can pull us down. We think of people, whose health has completely broken down due to some form of mental suffering. Those, who do not deal practically with such situations, would probably be surprised to know how many suffer through self-reproach. Few conditions wear down a person so quickly. It is difficult to shake off, and it prevents us from thinking straight. It can fill us with fear, so that we dread being alone, and at the same time we are half afraid of being with anyone, because we feel sure they think the same about us as we think of ourselves. We ought, therefore, to have great sympathy with those who suffer in this way. It is highly important to try to help those who are victims of self-reproach.

1 *Its futility*

When we suffer in this way we blame ourselves for something we have done or not done. It is nearly always the case that what we reproach ourselves for is something we have come to see in a different light. We should, however, make up our minds that, if we do the best we can at the time, even if it turns out badly, we are not going to reproach ourselves for not having acted differently.

When I was a small boy my father gave me a book, telling of the story of Captain Scott's dash for the South Pole, which surely must be one of the great stories of human endeavour and good faith. When the search party set out to try and find Scott and his men, they found them dead within a few miles of a relief post. Evans, one of the party, had been taken ill on the way back from the South Pole. What were they to do? Slow down and bring him along with them as far as they could; or leave him, perhaps with another man and some provisions, in the hope that a relief party would get to him in time? It was a terrible decision to have to make. They decided to bring Evans along with them, and it delayed their return; as it turned out, dangerously so. It meant that they ran into the bad weather that they would otherwise have encountered nearer base. It meant several days longer on the same provisions. As we all know now, they became too weak and exhausted to make good the delay, and they died in the Antarctic snows. The men, who had worked out the details of that gallant exploit so carefully, might have tortured themselves with self-reproach. They might have said that, if they had known then what they found out later on, they would have put down an extra provisions depot. But they had done the very best they could and there was very little that they could have done differently.

If we are going to allow ourselves to be tortured by self-reproach we shall never achieve anything, because we shall be afraid to attempt anything for fear that it turns out to be a failure. A decision is right or wrong at the time it is made, and we have to make our decisions according to the light that we have at the time. This needs to be said over and over again.

One of the most fruitful sources of self-reproach is in the memories we have of our loved ones, who have died. How often and how deeply we feel that we wish we had done differently! I have heard this said over and over again in my ministry. The little things come to mind. People dwell on them and they magnify them out of all proportion to the facts. But it is not only in relation to our loved ones, who have died, that so many of us reproach ourselves needlessly. It is also true of many of our friends, who are still living. I once had a very vivid experience of the sheer futility of self-reproach. There were some friends years ago, with whom I had a deep different of religious opinion, and for years I assumed that they would not want to listen to anything I might say to them any more. Some years later I discovered, quite by chance, that it had not struck them in the same way at all; in fact, they had forgotten everything about it. So, as well as having been very foolish, I had been unfair to them, by reproaching myself over something that was imaginary on my part.

2 *Its root and its remedy*

The truth is that self-reproach is really a form of pride. I would not say that if I could not say it from my own experience. We like to feel that all our actions and decisions are right, quite naturally, but, when they sometimes prove to be wrong, we feel aggrieved against ourselves for not having done better. We need constantly to remember that none of us is perfect—not yet anyway!—and we need to remember, too, that our fellow men are aware of that fact. We ought specially to remind ourselves that God knows it also. We are not omnipotent and it is to be expected that we shall make mistakes and errors of judgment in all sorts of ways; so we need the humility to admit the fact and to

166

be patient with ourselves, as well as with other people. We can but do right as we see the right, and for the rest we must trust to the goodness and mercy of God. If we are charitable and generous in our judgments—let this not be doubted—we shall find charity and generosity in our fellow men. This is certainly what I have found.

So, to those who are troubled and feel that, like Zacchaeus, they must hide themselves away, I would just say this: Take each day as it comes. At the beginning of it ask for God's help; at the middle of it remind yourself of what you asked at the beginning of the day; and at the end of the day look back over the day and entrust it to God, asking forgiveness for what has been wrong and thanking him for what has gone well—and so to bed, with a quiet mind.

3 Remorse—its near neighbour

I would like to add a word about something that is very much like self-reproach, but is quite a different thing. That is the question of remorse. Remorse belongs to a quite different level of experience. Remember that it is the conscientious who need to take steps against self-reproach; because we are human we are all apt to make mistakes, but God is ready to make good those failings. Remorse has to do, not with failings and mistakes; remorse belongs to those things we know to be wrong—things that we do deliberately, knowing them to be wrong, with our eyes open to the consequences of our action. In other words, the difference between remorse and self-reproach is the difference between deliberately wilful sin and simple human failings. If I may put it this way, it is the difference between what Judas Iscariot did and what Simon Peter did.

Simon Peter denied Christ, saying that he was nothing to him, when all the while he knew that the exact opposite was the truth, and he realized how much Christ meant to him. A moment later, when Christ turned and looked at Peter, Peter broke down and wept. But with Judas Iscariot, it was very different. Instead of trying to make out that Christ didn't mean much to him, he tried to make out that

167

he was his dearest friend; and, behind an outward show of loyalty and love (the kiss), Judas tried to hide his real intention. Long before it was all over Judas realized that he had done something that could never be undone. Christ's enemies now had him squarely in their hands, and they didn't bother about Judas any more. What Judas suffered was not self-reproach over his failings, but remorse for his sin. So there it is—there is a world of difference between remorse and self-reproach. Having said that, what can one say in a final word to those comparatively few, whose sufferings are remorse and not just self-reproach? Just this—and it is a wonderful thing to be able to say—there is no need for remorse for anything that can be forgiven. If we *want* forgiveness, it is there. Instead of allowing remorse to burn away the love from our hearts, we can go to God and let him see how deeply we are sorry for what was wrong. We can remember that, where there is love, there can always be forgiveness and peace.

PENTECOST 20

Falling away or building up

> Matthew 7.24 '*He is like a man who had the sense to build his house on rock.*'

It is easy to answer the question, 'Are you a Christian?' If you have been baptized in the name of the Father and the Son and the Holy Spirit, as Jesus told us in St Matthew 28.19, then you are a Christian. But it is not so easy to answer the question, 'Are you a good Christian?' Whereas Christian life and witness is something like the mercury in a barometer, sometimes it stands high and sometimes low according to the surrounding conditions, it is something like this with our faith and trust in God and our devotion to our Lord Jesus Christ. It has an up and down tendency; sometimes it stands higher and sometimes lower.

168

1 Falling away

It varies considerably even from day to day, though this must not be exaggerated, but over a long period, say a year or a number of years, there is in everyone an overall persistent falling away or an overall persistent rising up in the Christian faith and the Christian life. Nobody over a long term is static, staying on the same unshifting level of the Christian life year after year with no increase or deterioration. We used to be taught that nature abhors a vacuum. In the same way the Christian life abhors a static level.

The falling away process is too well known to need much comment, and it begins amongst the very youngest members of the Christian community. Even now in the present day Church, if every new Sunday School child remained faithful, then every church in the land would be crammed to capacity every Sunday; but it does not happen, because at every age some drop off until the old Christians are comparatively few. It is a cause for considerable reflection by most parish priests as to how few really Christian funerals they conduct.

Now this falling off in the Christian life is nothing new. Our Lord had a good deal to say about what to expect when the Christian life was found to be hard-going. St Paul complained to the Corinthians and again to the Galatians over precisely the same thing; and St John in the Book of Revelation, when writing to the small Christian communities in Asia Minor, particularly in Laodicea, tells of lukewarmness and a decreasing faith in those who were once glad and joyful converts. On the other hand, one sees in a few Christian souls the other process at work, the building-up process. There is, if one knows where to look for it, increasing achievement in the Christian life. It is to be seen in the classical sense in many older and faithful Christians and in many young ones, too, who are consciously placing their hands in the hand of God to lead them without reserve into some vocation or place of special service.

2 *Building up takes time*

There is then this process of increasing or decreasing. There cannot be one of us, who in his or her heart of hearts does not want to make good in the Christian life and to be on the side of the saints, but making this come true is a long-term policy. Indeed, the art of Christian living is probably the longest-term activity in which any man engages. It is, indeed, like the man who had the sense to build his house upon a rock, and it takes a lifetime of Christian living and devotion and worship to reproduce the character of Christ in some measure in any man. That is why the principal characteristics of the Christian are endurance and fortitude and a great patience in eucharistic worship and private devotion and other religious duties and almsgiving and all good works. This happens to be the way in which Christian living operates.

In Knaresborough in Yorkshire there is a well, in which the water has certain chemical properties. In the well are all manner of objects, like gloves and boots, which people have thrown in and left. If you go back after a day or two the object is not much changed, but if you go back after several months it has become encrusted and calcified, petrified into a stone glove or boot. This is because of the nature and property of the water. As the water drips down day by day the things in it partake of the nature of the water, to which they are constantly exposed, *but it takes a long time*.

So with the Christian life. Attendance at one celebration of the Holy Communion or one occasional prayer offered to God, when up against it, make little difference—we are much the same afterwards as before—but if we constantly present ourselves to the blessed sacrament, if we do not give up saying our prayers because it is hard, if we constantly expose ourselves to these unchanging holy influences of our Lord and build upon them, then we take on imperceptibly, at least in part, the nature of the Lord himself. It could hardly be otherwise. Here is the great value of a well-considered and regularly devised rule of life.

How easy it is to envy the person who has had some

170

sudden religious experience and who, because of it, became a fairly good Christian rather quickly. For most of us this just does not happen. Most of us were probably brought into contact with the Christian faith in early years and have never had any sudden religious experience. We know only too well all the slowness of the going in the Christian life and all the discouragements; but if we give Christ's body, the Church, a real chance, then we also find and know the very great comfort and heartwarming that comes from belonging to this body and building upon this rock with all its discipline, experience and sacrament of grace, and with its cheerful good company of likeminded Christian pilgrims.

PENTECOST 21

Bereavement

> John 11.21 *'If you had been here, sir, my brother would not have died.'*

1 The pain of bereavement

Here is a difficult story indeed for all facing bereavement, and today I want to speak to those who face this for the first time. Not that we ever get used to it, however often we have to face it; but the first experience can be terribly distressing. There is just that heavy heart, that awful gap, and that is all. Plenty of memories, but they come later; plenty of regrets, and if they come later rather than immediately then that is a mercy—but at first this indefinable pain, a pain that is not in your body but in *you*. As the first days go by we ought to find that we are getting less self-conscious about our bereavement, thinking less about how it affects *us*, and we begin to think of it in other ways. All our thoughts and questions about the hereafter, the future life and so on, all seem to come to this—'Where is he now?' 'What is she doing now?'

171

2 No ready-made answers

Quite frankly, one has to be very wary of people who claim to have a ready-made answer to these questions. Still less ought we to be induced to experiment with theories and practices that claim to put us in touch with our loved ones, who have died. We ought, I think, to be content with what Christ himself is content to tell us. He has not left us in the dark about anything that was necessary for us to know. If God wants us to be in touch with the departed spirits or if they were needing to get in touch with us, we can be sure that our Lord would show us the way. It has been the wisdom of the Church all down the ages simply to go on remembering them in prayer, believing that the mere fact of their being no longer with us in the body has not severed them from that wonderful communion and fellowship, of which Christ is the head.

3 Dying unrepentant

Another question that we find ourselves asking is this. Sometimes they have committed serious sins; and, so far as we know, they did not repent of them before they died. So we ask, in one form or another, the question: 'Shall we see our loved ones again?' 'Will he or she be forgiven?' I think that we must quite honestly say that there are serious differences of opinion about this. The truth is that there has been remarkable agreement among Christian people on one point. It is consistently held that repentance must begin in this life. But, having said that, quite emphatically we may say that we are not called upon to judge the repentance of another person. A priest may be called upon to hear an act of repentance, and to give help and encouragement; but it is God who judges, because he is the only one who knows.

It is difficult to deal with questions of this sort, simply because we find that we cannot lightly give easy words of assurance, when it looks as though we are flying in the face of facts. But we know this—God is love; and heaven must mean the exclusion of all evil, because God is love. As soon as we begin to realize our wrongdoing and to be genuinely penitent about it, there is full forgiveness for us. It may well be that this happens very gradually; that we enter step by step into the fullness of God. It is through God's forgiveness in all its fullness, but we enter into it gradually, as we become able to receive it.

So I believe we can ask ourselves, 'Are we quite sure that those, for whom we are anxious, have made no beginning towards this?' It may well be that in this life there was at some time a real turning from God. Again, our loved ones, who have died, are not placed beyond the reach of our prayers. Surely then, we are extremely unwise if we allow ourselves to be tortured by anxious fears. To be unduly apprehensive doesn't do them any good, and it certainly does us serious harm. Instead of allowing our faith and trust in God to be dissipated by these anxious fears, surely we ought to be using that faith and trust in quite simple ways, such as praying for our loved ones and devoting ourselves to some form of service to our fellow men.

4 Recognition of loved ones

We can say with confidence that we shall recognize our loved ones, but really we need a better word than 'recognize'. We recognize even a casual acquaintance. Christ teaches us that human nature is to be made perfect and what is bad in it is to be overcome with good. Once we get that in our minds it becomes a positively thrilling thing to realize that, provided we love what is good and true and beautiful, we shall love our loved ones and they will love us even more because they and we are being brought nearer and nearer to that perfect life. It follows that, when by God's mercy we and they are wholly good, we shall love one another in a way that excels even the highest happiness we know in this present life.

Conclusion

Sometimes, when I feel a little discouraged, I remind myself that nothing good will ever be lost. So, to all facing bereavement I would say, 'Let us try to remember that: Nothing good will ever be lost; only the evil will be kept out; and all goodness gathered in and made perfect in love.'

If we have these assurances, then we can turn quietly and confidently to our daily life, not reproaching ourselves for things that we cannot now alter, nor clinging to our grief and keeping on about it, but giving ourselves instead to the world's needs, because we have entrusted our loved ones to Christ.

PENTECOST 22

Fear of death

Luke 16.9 *'When money is a thing of the past you may be received into an eternal home.'*

Last Sunday we were thinking about bereavement, and especially when it comes to us for the first time; we go on now to think about the fear of death. Of course, the very word 'fear' almost makes us afraid, so we have to remind ourselves that fear isn't necessarily bad. There are some things that we should fear; it is good to fear dirt and disease, if it means that our fear of these things drives us into action against them. Many of us know from experience that to fear the loss of God's presence can be a fear that will result in nothing but good, if it helps us to choose what is good and what is right, especially when what we want isn't what is good for us. There is also what the Bible calls 'the fear of God', and that is really another way of describing what we mean by reverence. We all know well that we fear to hurt one whom we love. So obviously it is really *what* we fear, rather than fear itself, that we need to think about.

174

1 Stepping into the unknown

It is worth remembering that worry or anxiety are different forms of fear. It is quite possible that what we think of as fear is not so much a real fear of death, but just that the thought of it worries us and makes us anxious; and that is most probably because we may have entirely the wrong idea about death. You may well have heard someone say, 'I am not afraid to die.' I think it is tremendously impressive that, of all the people I have known who have suffered from some incurable disease, I can hardly think of one who was afraid to die. Nature has a most wonderful way of preparing us for the next step, and that is really what death is—the next step—a step into the unknown.

When we are young we love adventures; we like to explore unknown woods, to roam over the hills, to discover fresh scenery and to meet new people. Usually, as the years roll by we lose something of this love. We tend to prefer familiar scenes and to turn to those friends whom we have proven through the years. Death means for so many people the loss of things that we are used to; the separation from friends and loved ones; the turning away from old familiar scenes. It can be this that makes us afraid. It is as though death comes and leads us away from it all, and we have to take a step into the unknown, from which there is no turning back.

2 The difference the Christian faith makes

Now it is here that we find what an enormous difference the Christian religion can make. For the Christian, death is not simply a step into the unknown. We shall go to Christ, and he will talk to us about the life we have lived and the sort of person we are. Now that would be something to fear if we are ashamed of the life we have lived and the sort of person we are; and it would certainly be something to fear if we ought to be ashamed and we are not. If we really are trying to do our best with God's help to be the sort of person that Christ can make us, and to live the kind of life that really does remind people of Christ (simply because there is love and warmth and generosity about it)—in these circumstances, there is simply nothing of which to be afraid.

For the person who doesn't believe the Christian faith, death sometimes seems a very cruel thing. It cuts him off from everything that he has thought so much about and disposes of him. What a prospect!—as if life's hopes and joys are to come to this! To go through life trying to be helpful, trying to do something really worthwhile, and to learn to love what is good and beautiful, only to have it cut short and thrown aside as useless! But, many might say, you cannot deny that we are disposed of. I *do* deny it quite emphatically; for there is all the difference in the world between disposing of *us* and disposing of our mortal remains.

3 *Our mortal remains*

When death comes, it means that our body has served its purpose and that this body is not now required and dies. Our real self, the living person, comes to Christ. Sometimes death is spoken of as 'crossing the river'. Suppose we are crossing a river, we are the same person when we get to the other side. Something very wonderful has happened to us, but we are still ourselves. So whether we think of it as taking a step into the unknown or whether we think of it as 'crossing the river', there is absolutely nothing of which to be afraid.

To many it seems incredible that we could have any real existence without our body, and that may be all the more difficult when we have given so much time and thought to the needs and comforts of our body. There may well be a real lesson here, for why do we give so much care and attention to the bodily parts of our nature and so little comparatively to the mental and spiritual parts?

Don't let us worry about what is going to happen to our body when we have left it. If it has been troublesome, it may be all the easier to have done with it! It has been said

176

that the body can be a good servant but a bad master. We ought not to think of it in that way. When death comes we shall leave our body. If it has been a good servant, and it probably will have been if we have used it wisely and well, especially if we have been blessed with good health—then well and good; but if not, then we shall be free of it. In either case we shall come to Christ; and that is what matters. We don't go down into darkness; we come to Christ. Instead, therefore, of allowing ourselves to dread death, think of our coming to Christ, and try and do what we can to become the kind of person who can quietly look forward to a welcome from him, when we come to him.

LAST SUNDAY AFTER PENTECOST

Perfection

Matthew 25.13 *'Keep awake then; for you never know the day or the hour.'*

Critical and intelligent readers of the New Testament, who know their book really well, alarm and discourage many of us by saying that the New Testament has not the slightest interest in what may be called amateur Christianity. By amateur they mean part-time work. They go on to point out that it is professional Christianity, declared and whole-time loyalty, with which the New Testament is concerned. We must not press the analogy too far because, for instance, in cricket some amateurs are better than some professionals. But the simile is able to carry enough truth for anyone to know what is meant. Nominal Christianity, Sunday Christians, sporadic worshippers, good pagans, who are really quite decent in their own queer way—the New Testament displays no interest whatsoever in such things; on the contrary the New Testament is deeply concerned with the eventual perfection of redeemed human characters in Christ.

1 *Perfection—a basic New Testament theme*

Now this theme of absolute perfection is not occasional and incidental in New Testament thought, but it seems to be part of its main structure. For instance, Jesus himself in the much-invoked but seldom-read sermon on the mount said: 'Be perfect as your Father in heaven is perfect.' To a well-heeled young man, who was reluctant to part with cash and chattels, Jesus pointed out that they were the main obstacle in his particular case to be got rid of '*if you will be perfect.*' Twenty-four hours before his death, Jesus was found praying for his somewhat slow and far from reliable disciples, asking '*they may be made perfect.*'

Then Paul, writing to the Christians in Ephesus, points out that the more each one of us imitates Jesus, the nearer he will come to being *a perfect man*, the measure of the stature of the fullness of Christ. Then James, in his letter, is found praying that his correspondent *may be perfect and entire, wanting nothing.* The unknown author, who wrote the letter to the Hebrews, advises his much more Christianly advanced readers to pass on from elementary stages and to go on *to perfection.* Furthermore, Peter and John constantly emphasize the same theme, saying in effect: 'Have no truck with half-measures. Do not play about with the Christian faith. Throw all you have into it or else throw it up altogether.' Part-time Christianity is nowhere mentioned in the New Testament.

2 *Encouragement for beginners*

In saying this, the New Testament writers are not setting themselves up to be pious immaculates nor to discourage beginners in the faith. They are not being heavy-handed with those who are finding the Christian life hard going. On the contrary, beginners in the Christian faith receive constant encouragement all the way through the New Testament; but not those individuals, who bestir themselves sufficiently to go into the fellowship of the Church, and then, as it were, sit down just inside the door with no intention, or even thought, of making any further spiritual progress.

So the Church's work is not only to bring outsiders *in*, but also insiders *on*. By instruction, by encouragement and by precept we are all constantly to be encouraging all old-timers, as well as newcomers, to progress in the Christian life, to increase in the appreciation of God, to better prayers, better worship, better witness. In a word, to press on towards the perfection, which is to Christ himself, whom all we ourselves know only in part, and each man and woman according to one's own progress. One of the chief ways in which people have first been attracted to the Christian religion is by an intelligent reading of the New Testament. During this process it has dawned upon many a good pagan that Christianity is not mere good humour, gentle behaviour and tolerant amiability. Christianity is centred upon the personality of Jesus of Nazareth, whom we confess as the Christ, and who was done to death but rose again.

3 *Conclusion*

These are the facts of history, upon which the faith is founded, and from which no one calling himself a Christian can be free. So our religion does not consist of vague sentiment and advice about being good. It consists of certain actions of God, which he carried out at a certain place and time in our history, 'for us men and for our salvation.' That is why the Christian minority has never been in the insidious position of having to say to outsiders: 'You ought to try and be like us.' The burden of what Christians must say is: 'We ought to be like Christ himself.' The Christian target is nothing short of perfection—the Lord himself.

179